GARDEN COLOUR SERIES

WATER GARDENING

Frances Perry

AURA
EDITIONS

Endpaper *The brilliant, crimson-red blooms of the water-lily, Nymphaea 'Escarboucle'.*

Facing title page *The charm and informality of this garden pool is deceptive: only by careful planning and regular care can such a lush and healthy environment be provided for both fish and plant life.*

Right *By imaginative use of brick, granite, concrete and water, a shady town garden has been transformed into a 'country' retreat of style and character.*

Series Editor: Susan Conder
Editor: Eluned James
Art Editor: Caroline Dewing

Published by
Aura Editions
2 Derby Road
Greenford, Middlesex

Produced by Marshall Cavendish Books Ltd
58 Old Compton Street
London W1V 5PA

ISBN 0 86307 277 1

Typeset in Ehrhardt 453 by Walkergate Press, Anlaby
Printed and bound in Hong Kong by Dai Nippon
Printing Company

CONTENTS

INTRODUCTION

No matter how complete your garden seems, the inclusion of a pool will bring to it the music and movement of water and a new world of plants and wildlife for you to enjoy.

Opposite *The water surrounding Wakehurst Place, Sussex reflects the beautiful autumnal colours of the trees and shrubs.*

Below *Over the centuries, the grace and beauty of water gardens has led to some spectacular creations. Here, the cascading waterfall and fountains of the Villa d'Este, in Tivoli – a gem of the Italian Renaissance – are enhanced by elegant balustrades and classical statuary.*

The use of water as an ornamental feature in gardens has only become popular in Britain this century. Before that it was difficult to build pools which did not leak. Some people grew water-lilies in lead or zinc tanks or old household baths, but these often proved unsatisfactory as few understood the importance of correct siting, the effect of lead and the like on fish and the interdependence of plant and animal life necessary to ensure water clarity. Nor were there enough attractive water plants available to impel many gardeners to make the effort, although it is true that there were numbers of large estates with natural lakes. Many of these were spangled with white water-lilies in summer and possibly had yellow water irises and pink flowering rushes growing in the shallows. However, few suburban gardens and virtually no townsfolk owned attractive pools.

It was otherwise abroad, where the aesthetic qualities of water have long been recognized. The Hanging Gardens of Babylon reputedly owed much of their fame to the uses made of water; the Egyptians designed pools for growing lotuses and papyrus; there are water features around the Taj Mahal in India, while the fountain gardens of Versailles have attracted millions since their construction in the 17th century. We know, too, that the Romans loved running water, while nowadays their descendants, along with Spaniards and Portuguese as well as various South American countries at one time colonized by these Europeans, build their homes around water features in a central courtyard. In hot climates, playing water instils a sense of peace and coolness.

Several factors changed the neglect of water features in Britain, first to interest and then enthusiasm. Originally it was the large-scale use of concrete, which allowed strong pools to be made to any size and shape, raised above the ground or sunken and in any garden. But these proved to be fairly expensive, and leaked if not properly made. Also their construction involved much hard work – this was before the days of pre-mixed concrete and, once built, could not easily be removed. However, in spite of these drawbacks many were made, especially between the wars, when it became almost a status symbol to have a pool in your garden.

Another event which contributed to their popularity was the arrival from France at the turn of the century of a great number of water-lilies, and the wealth of colours they displayed amazed connoisseurs. No longer was it necessary to stick to white water-lilies, for now there were various shades of pinks and reds, creams and even yellows available, also large, medium-sized and miniature varieties for pools of different depths. Then, after World War II, plastics became more readily available and suddenly everyone who wanted a water garden found it possible, sometimes in a matter of hours, to have one.

Besides bringing an indefinable quality to gardening, the presence of water has many visual attractions. As well as providing a means to grow plants which would not succeed anywhere else, it attracts life in many forms. Darting fish of various colours bring movement and animation in the pool itself, while birds, bees and butterflies wing their way to its margins in search of water, and frogs, newts and toads are all attracted to water at breeding time.

The reflective properties of water provide an important bonus, duplicating the charms of nearby plants and trees. It will also mirror the clouds on a spring day or the blue of a summer sky, while the pattern of its surface changes with the weather – rippling in miniature waves during a high wind, sparkling in sunshine, becoming dark and sombre prior to a storm, and literally jumping in staccato jerks when raindrops fall. Even in winter, water is not without charm, especially when stray shafts of sunlight cause the surface of an ice covered pool to sparkle with flashing lights or frost appears on the dead stems of nearby vegetation.

There is still another attribute to water in the garden. When it moves, it creates various musical sounds and even the reeds, grasses and sedges which thrive in the vicinity of water have a musical quality when rustled by wind or disturbed by birds. Bamboos particularly, make a whispering noise, rather like the murmur of village gossips heard at a distance. All these mixed notes create sounds which contribute to the air of liveliness and enjoyment which can be experienced by those who include water features in their garden.

CHAPTER 1

CHOOSING A POOL

Before deciding on the kind of pool you want, consider the alternatives carefully. There are numerous possibilities for even the smallest space and you may find an option you had not thought of for your garden.

Whichever type of pool you decide to build certain principles have to be borne in mind when dealing with water as a garden feature. It should never be used in an unnatural place, for example perched on top of a hill where it would never occur in nature, and it must receive plenty of sunshine. This is imperative even if you only intend to use the pool to reflect light and clouds. In the case of a planted pool, lack of sunshine inhibits flowering and virtually no aquatics will bloom in shade.

The pool should also be well away from overhanging trees, although the protection of a building or trees in the background towards the east or north, could be an asset in a cold spring.

It is also advantageous to be within easy distance of a source of piped water, also electricity if lighting is contemplated or a pump is to be installed to circulate the water for a waterfall or fountain.

Finally, in order to enjoy the peace and quiet generated by water it is advisable to build all water features as far away as possible from the noise and pollution of busy main roads.

Buying or building?

To buy or to build? This is a question all who want a water garden must decide for themselves. Undoubtedly the first alternative will prove the most expensive but if time or physical strength matter it may have to be considered. Or, if you want a large concrete structure it may be the only answer.

However, it is not difficult to construct a small pool, especially if you use modern materials, nor need it be prohibitively expensive. The thing to do is consider the alternatives; first the pool site and its size, then its nature, formal or informal, next the fabric – concrete, prefabricated or plastic sheeting and finally possible extras such as fountains and waterfalls. With all this decided then make a plan, decide how much you are prepared to do yourself – excavation can be hard and heavy, also concreting – then shop around for the materials and be ready to adjust your calculations when you know the prices of each item you want.

Making the most of natural features

Very few gardeners are lucky enough to have natural water in the form of a pond or stream on their property, but where it does occur, the best way of treating it is to incorporate it into an informal landscape design. This course of action has been eminently successful with many great gardens of the past, such as the lakes of Stourhead and Blenheim, or the peaceful river setting at Wilton and the Cambridge Backs, where the misty effect of budding willows and riverside gardens is reflected in the moving waters of the Cam.

The peaceful countryside of Britain is only rarely parched with drought, unlike the warmer lands of southern Europe where the coolness engendered by playing fountains is particularly welcome. In hot climates you cannot have too much water and the sound and sight of droplets constantly falling refreshes one's spirits and cools the air around. In Britain, however, there are too many dull days for fountains – with their reminders of rain – to be continually playing, and when natural water is present you can enjoy its movement and reflective properties in quieter fashion, simply by copying nature. Thus rock and water team delightfully and, if a source of local stone is available, this could prove the happiest of marriages. Height can be obtained by building up parts of the garden with soil and rocks, particularly useful in cases where the flow of water is fast as it enables it to find its way downwards in a series of falls to lakes or ponds beyond. A partnership of rock and water also enables you to grow a varied collection of plants; alpines and aquatics, moisture lovers and kinds which appreciate sharp drainage. Small areas of grass and occasional outcrops of stone, the odd shrub or tree will also fit naturally into such schemes.

If the stream or river is wide enough to merit a bridge, this can be built to make an interesting focal point. An informal stone bridge of Japanese design, constructed of oblong blocks of stone set diagonally on a strong base would be attractive in a woodland setting, especially if the bank was

The most successful pools are often designed around natural features. Here, terraces have been cut into a sloping site to produce a series of fast-moving falls, while the rocky surrounds shelter moisture-loving plants like the Candelabra primulas in the foreground.

Instead of a single pond, this garden has two matching pools, each given height and interest by the inclusion of a fountain. The pools are linked visually by their complementary designs and, physically, by a small rustic bridge which blends with the nearby trees.

planted with bog primulas, ferns, bluebells and other moisture-loving shade plants. In a more open situation, a rustic bridge might be more appropriate, especially when draped with wisteria, after the fashion of the one in the Royal Horticultural Society's Garden at Wisley.

Again, by damming or diverting a stream it is possible not only to form small cascades through rocks but also to fill large pools. Much ingenuity, however, is necessary if water is to be diverted, so it is advisable to work out a plan on paper first. Points to consider include the nature of the surrounding soil. If it is heavy clay it may be possible to puddle it to render the diversion watertight, but more probably it will be of a porous nature in which case you either risk losing the water, or flooding adjacent land. With small diversions the new area could

probably be lined with concrete or plastic sheeting in order to retain the water.

Summer droughts can also cause problems, adversely affecting both fish and plants. A simple way of reducing the flow of a stream or river away from the garden is to install a few stepping stones. This will slow it down without stopping its movement.

The law gives the riverside gardener certain rights but also imposes a number of obligations. He may use the water for normal home or garden purposes and is permitted to build up its banks to control flooding, but he must not materially affect its flow. Granted the right to enjoy flowing water through his property, he also has the right to let it flow away without hindrance to other properties. However, these rules do not apply to artificial waters such as canals and reservoirs. If in doubt on any of these points, consult your local Regional Water Authority before undertaking any alterations.

Finally, cattle ponds are frequently found on older properties, often filled with years of debris. These should be emptied and cleaned before being planted, a laborious task, although there are firms which undertake dredging if required.

Artificial pools

In many respects, artificial pools are easier to manage and offer more scope to the gardener than existing sources of water. For one thing, natural water may not be

where you want it and, although it is possible to get rid of a small disused pond, it is not so easy in the case of streams or rivers.

An artificial pool, on the other hand, can be controlled as regards size, depth and shape, and built to fit any size of garden or planting scheme. The important thing is to ensure that it fits in with the surrounds. In other words, it should be right for the position it is to occupy. The main feature of any water garden is accumulated water, either in the shape of a pond or stream – possibly with the added attraction of a waterfall, cascade or fountain. All of these can be simulated using modern materials.

No attempt has been made to hide the artificial nature of this water garden. The strictly formal lines are emphasized by neatly grouped plants and simple jets of water are used to carry the eye towards the focal point – an exotic statue fringed by bamboos.

Below *Round paving units harmonize with the circular, raised brick pool while pot plants and flower beds provide a splash of colour.*

Formal pools

A formal pool is one that is patently artificial. The aim is to create a focal point, a place to rest or 'stop and stare'. Usually it will be constructed to some geometric design such as a circle, square, half-moon or an oblong. A formal pool can either be sunk into the ground or have its sides raised to form a curb. According to preference, this curb can be quite low or fairly high and have its upper surface left flat or sloping. Some people mould the tops into scallops or other designs, perhaps repeating a pattern similar to one found round the base of a statue or fountain standing inside the pool. Curbs were occasionally built high enough to provide a seat, so that people could sit and watch and feed the fish or view the water-lilies in comfort. Indeed, low walls with a flat stone coping are often seen around modern pools for the same reasons.

Naturally, any pool with a raised coping has to be substantially constructed or it could become dangerous. For this reason they are usually made of concrete or brick faced with concrete.

In the case of a sunken pool, a border of firm paving stones provides a neat finish, especially if the pool stands in an open position, as on a lawn. This invites people to walk up to it and also provides a steady base on which to stand containers of plants.

One idea is to make the pool in the centre of a sunken plot, building it to the same shape as the surround. Thus an oblong pool would lie in the middle of an oblong plot, a circular pool in a round area and so on. Apart from the pool, all of this would be paved, although the sides could be built up with raised beds or possibly a wall and steps. The wall could be built of bricks or treated as a dry wall with yellow alyssum, campanulas, rock phlox and aubrietas trailing down between the stones. A sunken

garden of this type would make a splendid suntrap and, by fending off strong winds, would quickly become a popular retreat for much of the year.

Basin pools
These are popular in small town gardens where the presence of water is desired but not the upkeep of a planted pool. If you do not intend to keep fish or grow plants, make or purchase a round concrete container and fill it with large pebbles. Introduce water in the form of a spring or gusher and allow the water to bubble up through the stones. A pump ensures that the same water is used over and over again.

Another idea is to install a pair of these spouting bowls, one each side of a doorway leading from the house into the garden, but far enough forward to allow people to walk freely without getting wet. If the bowls have a small area of soil left around them and the

rest is paved, it will be possible to plant pansies, forget-me-nots or dwarf bedding begonias as a foil for the water.

Wall fountains
Another method of enjoying water in a small garden is by building a small formal pool close to a boundary wall and playing water into the pool via a fountain. This is usually fixed to the wall; an animal's stone head is frequently used for the purpose. Alternatively, a spouting dolphin or similar figure can be placed inside the pool; the water kept moving and returned by means of a pump.

Informal pools
Just as a formal pool is only appropriate to a formal surround, so one designed to be informal must fit in with a natural-looking background. It must also be built at the lowest point of the garden, otherwise it

Above left *A circular pool provides interest in this town garden. Spaces in the paved area have been planted with hostas, ivy and* Impatiens sultani, *a busy Lizzie with delicate, pale blooms.*

Above *In this low-maintenance garden, the pool is the most important feature. Its delightful fountain is framed with the bright yellow and green of* Caltha palustris, *the marsh marigold.*

In this classical Japanese design, a curved wooden bridge spans still waters and peaceful vistas lie around each corner. The whole scene is cut off from the outside world by judicious planting of trees.

ceases to be natural, for water always finds its own level. The liberties sometimes taken with formal pools, which are placed at unusual heights or in curious situations for effect, are completely inappropriate for informal water gardens.

Rock and water

Although water occurs in various situations in nature, such as in fields or woods adjacent to hedgerows or among rocks, the rocky site undoubtedly creates the most impressive effects. An informal pool, surrounded by rocks, attains a touch of grandeur but natural rock is hard to come by and, not surprisingly, some local authorities are now preventing its removal from unspoiled sites. Artificial rock can never match it, although as time goes by this may improve. However, there are still some sources of stone if you shop around.

One benefit of teaming rock with water is that the soil excavated when the pool is made does not have to be removed. Instead it can be built up to give height and also

provide facilities for installing a waterfall as well as rocks.

A Japanese effect

On reasonably large sites a water feature which is becoming increasingly popular is a garden in the Japanese style. Here water, stones, plants, trees, bridges and ornaments all have a place. Free use is made of stones leading across water to a small teahouse or a stone ornament. Japanese gardens are quiet gardens, never ablaze with colour but mostly in shades of green, yet indescribably beautiful and peaceful.

Bog and water

An informal pool with connecting bog garden is another idea. This is particularly appropriate for gardens which normally lie wet, for bogs help to drain surplus water from surrounding land. It also provides a place to grow those plants which must be constantly moist at their roots.

At its simplest, a bog is merely a low lying area prone to collect water. It can be constructed artificially by excavating and lining a basin about 23cm (9in) deep with plastic sheeting. Cover the base with a layer of stones or broken bricks to trap some water, then return the soil with added rotted compost and more soil to a depth of 30cm (12in). Try to avoid very sharp stones which might puncture the sheeting. The level of the soil should then be about 7.5cm (3in) above the liner. Thus the top layer of soil can drain fairly freely so that the bog area is moist but not waterlogged.

Occasionally a bog garden may have to be subdivided into sections, simply because different conditions occur in different parts of the same garden. There could, for instance, be a spot which, although in full sunshine, is perpetually wet. Not every plant would appreciate this but it would be ideal for *Iris kaempferi*, calthas, acorus and ligularias; that is, plants which will tolerate standing in water for longish periods.

However, in order to ensure that it does not become so wet that it is constantly waterlogged, the topsoil may have to be built up above the level of standing water. The roots would then remain damp, but not the crowns of the plants.

This will be the preliminary for the main section of bog and will be similar to the conditions found along the banks of a stream. In this case, 30cm (12in) of topsoil enriched with organic matter is desirable and, if the site becomes dry, water can be added with a hose or by flooding over the pool. Many plants will thrive in this section, including astilbes, bog primulas, day lilies *(Hemerocallis)*, trollius, water forget-me-nots, mimulus, and rodgersias.

The last section only applies to sites which are heavily shaded. Less spectacular effects are to be expected but among a number of plants likely to succeed are bamboos, flag irises and willows.

A highlight of any visit to Bressingham Hall in Norfolk is the informal pool and its colourful selection of bog and water plants. A thatched garden house built of local flint looks out over the scene and complements the rustic mood.

CHAPTER 2

BUILDING A POOL

Whether you buy a pre-fabricated pool, use a simple liner or build a more ambitious concrete structure, there are a few basic guidelines you should follow to avoid disasters and ensure success.

There are various ways of building a pool and it is only sensible to consider all the options before rushing into action.

If, for instance, you only want a modest shallow receptacle, purely for ornament rather than for growing plants, there is no need to build a huge concrete structure. Instead, an appearance of strength and permanence can be obtained very simply, by providing an edging of paving stones to a sunken pool, made of nothing more robust than a polythene sheeting liner.

On the other hand, an elaborate water garden, destined to hold deep-water aquatics, will inevitably involve a heavy weight of water, especially if there are to be ornamental additions, such as an impressive fountain, placing an extra strain on the base. The pool in this case will have to be strong and almost certainly built of concrete.

Preliminaries

Another early consideration will be the source of the water supply. If this comes from a stream or other natural source, the flow is likely to fluctuate, especially in a drought, after snow or a heavy thunder storm. You are really safer with piped water and, in any case, the pool should be within easy reach of same. Pools do need topping up from time to time and may also have to be flooded over occasionally in order to remove floating scum, flower petals and similar debris. It may also be necessary to channel water into a bog garden.

However, once the pool is built and planted, it should not be necessary to keep changing the water. This is an impetuous reaction by gardeners when the water turns green or cloudy soon after planting. But it is a mistake, for some initial cloudiness is inevitable. Everything about a new pool is raw and immature.

The soil is fresh, the plants barely rooted and the water – maybe containing chemicals – has come straight out of a tap. It takes time for all these things to adjust but, gradually, as the plants root into the mud and the oxygenators, in particular, increase, the water clears. It may be advisable to flood the pool over once to remove scum

and loose debris but after that leave it alone to settle. The aim is to obtain still, 'matured' water similar to that found in clear lakes or undisturbed ponds.

In these early stages some thought should be given to the positioning of the water garden, especially its proximity to sources of pollution. This may be caused by a number of things, such as seepage from surface water from a busy road containing perhaps oil or petrol, even sewage or, in the case of a stream or river, the water may be affected by effluent from a factory site farther back. It is much better to find out about these things before starting to build than suffer constant aggravation later on.

Having decided on the type of pool you want, formal or informal, satisfy yourself that the surrounds are suitable and then decide on its size and shape. This is sometimes difficult to assess so it is a good idea to obtain an old clothes line or a length of rope and lay this on the ground, so that it roughly outlines the proposed shape. View the result from all angles, including an upstairs room if the pool will be in constant view from the house, and move the rope about until you are satisfied with the result. Next, secure the shape to act as a guide during excavation, either by knocking in pegs or, with a spade, notch a shallow trench in the soil to follow the outline of the rope.

What depth?

An informal pool will probably need to be made in several depths 60–75cm (24–30in) for the area where fish, oxygenators and water-lilies will be living, but a fairly shallow area 20cm (8in) for marginal water plants. Most of the latter only need to have their roots submerged, leaving the stems, flowers and leaves free to grow above the surface.

Dealing with the deeper parts first, you must consider the options. There are water-lilies which need a good depth of water, which means an excavation of 75cm (30in), allowing 15cm (6in) for the container in which they are planted and 60cm (24in) of water. The majority of lilies, however, are best in water 30–45cm (12–

When building a pool, it is worth looking at its setting and the surrounding area to see what additions you could make. Here, a rockery and waterfall combine to add a new dimension to the original plan.

18in) above their containers, which means an overall depth of 45–60cm (18–24in). At these depths a complete freeze-up in winter is rarely a problem. Ice may form but not so severely as to threaten the water-lilies or fish and in any case there are precautions one can take. Accordingly, it is rarely necessary to excavate any deeper. It makes a lot of extra work to remove a further foot or so of soil, not to mention problems arising as to its disposal. Also, when the pool is eventually filled with water, very few water-lilies are able to negotiate a depth of 1–1.1m (3–3½ft) as sometimes recommended, particularly the coloured sorts. Water in a deep pool will also be much colder than in a shallow one.

Remember, too, that water flowing into a pool from a spring or stream will be constantly changing, gaining and losing water all the time. It will accordingly be cooler than static water in a pool that was originally run in from a tap, a circumstance which will not only make flowering late but probably reduce the quantity of bloom. Since water-lilies in any case do not like running water, it is advisable to plant only vigorous kinds (regardless of depth) where there is water movement.

Clay pools

Clay or dew pools, the last name referring to the fact that dews contributed to their water content, were probably the first pools to be constructed in Britain. They were mainly built and used by country folk for watering stock, although, towards the end of the nineteenth century, a number were constructed to house ornamental plants and fish.

However, the construction of a clay pool in the past was normally messy and difficult, and involved lining an excavated cavity with a good layer of coarse straw, although sometimes heather was used, topped by a thick stratum of clay. The latter was kept damp and kneaded into the straw with the aid of heavy pressure from rollers or sometimes trampling horses. Later it was smoothed over and filled with water. Normally after that, dews condensing on the cold clay, plus leakage from land drains kept it topped up, which was important to prevent cracks and subsequent leakage. Small wonder people welcomed the arrival of concrete as an alternative to the effort of making puddled clay.

For some sixty years concrete pools held the market, until the coming of plastics changed things yet again. Nowadays, small to medium-sized pools are generally made either by using prefabricated shells or by lining a cavity with plastic sheeting. However, for building pools with raised sides or those constructed in places where seepage occurs or vandals can damage plastic, concrete is still popular.

Making a concrete pool

There are advantages and disadvantages in using concrete for pool making. On the credit side, it is strong and durable and can be made to any design, including raised structures. Disadvantages include expense,

When mixing your own concrete, it is important to get the correct consistency. The most common mistake is to add too much water, leaving puddles in the mix: the correct proportions will result in a smooth consistency, as shown here.

the labour of laying and possibly mixing concrete and the fact that, once installed, concrete is difficult to remove. Also, if, for any reason, cracks appear, it will probably leak and have to be emptied and mended.

However, if you do decide to use concrete, you will find it easier to make the deepest part – which is where the fish and water-lilies will be – to a conventional shape, such as a square or rectangle. Make the walls of this section slope inwards, to an angle of approximately 20 degrees, so that the widest part is at the top. This will lessen any pressure caused by expanding ice in winter – a common cause of cracks.

This need not remain the final shape, especially if you prefer an informal pool. After the deep part is finished, construct a marginal trough all round its extremities 30cm (12in) deep but any shape you favour. This depth allows for 10cm (4in) of concrete and 10cm (4in) each of soil and water, which is ideal for most marginal aquatics. It is important to make the outer edge of the trough 2.5cm (1in) higher than the sides of the inner pool, so that when full of water this can flow over to the outer extremities and effectively disguise the fact that there is an inside part. The final height of the inner, symmetrical walls, will be 2.5cm (1in) below the surface of the water. This method will also make the pool look larger than it really is.

When taking out soil for the deep section, it is important to remember to add 15cm (6in) to all measurements. This is the thickness of concrete necessary to counteract the effects both of heavy traffic and hard winters. Thus a pool designed to be $1.8 \times 1.2 \times 0.4$m ($6 \times 4 \times 1\frac{1}{2}$ft) deep should be excavated to $1.95 \times 1.35 \times 0.6$m ($6\frac{1}{2} \times 4\frac{1}{2} \times 2$ft).

Unless the intention is to use ready-mixed concrete you will need to make your own from best Portland cement, sharp builder's sand and clean aggregate (gravel or ballast) which is free from organic particles and grading from 5–20mm ($\frac{3}{16}$ to $\frac{3}{4}$ inch in the proportions of 1:2:3 (by volume – not weight). These ingredients, after being thoroughly mixed dry, should have water added to bind them, gently – not squirted through a powerful jet – after which the heap should be turned a couple of times. It is impossible to overmix concrete but very easy to add too much water, so take care. Enough should be added so that, when tested by having a shovel thrust into the heap, then drawn in and out in a series of jerks, the resulting ridges should retain their shape without settling back in a sloppy mess. Only if the ingredients are properly mixed will the blend be strong.

For any pool larger than 1.2m (4ft) square, it is a good idea to introduce some kind of reinforcement, such as galvanized wire mesh and/or expanded metal laths obtained from a builder. This gives it added strength. Before concreting, make sure that the base is firm and level, filling in cavities with hardcore if necessary. Then lay the base, applying 15cm (6in) for a small pool or, if reinforcement is to be introduced, 7.5cm (3in). The reinforcement should be laid on this while the concrete is still moist, leaving enough all round, turned up at the edges, to cast into the walls. When this is done, apply a further 7.5cm (3in) of concrete on top. This accounts for the base but, before the concrete is quite set, scratch mark the surface to a width of 15cm (6in) all round the sides, thus leaving a rough face to facilitate the joins when the sides are made.

To hold the sides while the concrete is setting, the best plan is to introduce

Making concrete is a fairly straightforward task:
1 For successful results, use ingredients of the best possible quality. Make sure that the sand and aggregate are clean and measure them carefully to the right proportions (see this page).
2 Mix the ingredients together while they are still dry, then make a crater in the centre of the heap.
3 Pour in a measured quantity of clean water.
4 Mix thoroughly, until the right consistency is achieved.

An edging of paving stones around a pool not only provides a firm footing for passers-by, it also prevents soil from crumbling into the water. The statue of a heron serves a dual purpose, too: it makes an elegant pool-side feature and, at the same time, deters real herons from coming to steal the fish.

shuttering. This takes the form of a roofless, bottomless wooden 'box' made out of boards and just 15cm (6in) shorter on all its sides than the actual pool measurements.

When making the sides, work round and round, paying particular attention to the corners.

A few days later you should, waterproof the pool and seal off the harmful free lime (which is always present in new concrete and adversely affects fish) by painting a proprietary compound all over the walls and floor.

Prefabricated pools

Prefabricated pools came in around the 1940s and found instant appeal, especially with town and suburban gardeners. In 1940, the idea of a portable pool was conceived and several were made, of a round and oblong shape, from the only material then available – aluminium. Even aluminium was in short supply at the time, but then plastics were invented and, after the war others took up the idea, using this versatile new material.

Through the years they have been steadily improved and now are either made of semi-rigid plastic or of fibreglass bonded with polyester resins; the latter being the toughest and also the most expensive. Designs, too, have developed so that today it is possible to obtain circular, oblong, square and crescent-shaped pools as well as irregular shapes which are more suitable for informal water gardens. Some of the latter may be as much as 3.5m (11½ft) long, one, at least, having two deep pools linked by shallower areas between.

Many have punched-out areas of different depths so that plants in pots can be stood on them and receive the right amount of water over their roots. This is especially useful when growing marginal aquatics.

Some have inconspicuous plain edges so that they can be set unobtrusively in the ground and look quite natural. This is ideal for pools teamed with rock gardens, or having bog surrounds. Other prefabricated pools have obviously artificial rims, simulating rocks or paving stones. One round pool, for example, 1.85m (6ft 2in) in diameter and with approximately half its area 45cm (18in) deep and the rest 23cm (9in), is finished with a broad outer rim, marked into sections to represent paving stones. This would make a suitable pool for a key position in a formal area.

Although most garden centres have stocks of prefabricated pools, the most comprehensive collections are to be found in nurseries or centres which specialize in aquatic features.

Although some centres stock the flimsier semi-rigid, pre-formed pools of weather-resistant plastic, these cannot compare for strength or durability with the heavier fibreglass kinds. Admittedly, they are cheaper but there are fewer designs available. They also tend to buckle and, being somewhat fragile, are more liable to damage from sharp instruments. Repair kits are available for both these and fibreglass pools, but there is far less likelihood of them being needed for fibreglass than for weather-resistant plastic.

Installation

To install a prefabricated pool you must first take out sufficient soil to enable it to sit inside comfortably, plus an extra 15cm (6in)

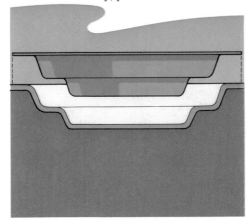

all around the sides. Next, firm the base and cover it with an inch of sand, sifted soil or ashes, then stand the pool in place and test it for levels. Use a spirit level for this, as it is important to get this point settled right at the outset, otherwise the water will run to one end when the pool is filled. Once the pool is planted, it will be impossible to alter things and its unevenness will become a recurring source of annoyance.

Now run in a little water to hold the pool steady while you backfill soil all around the edges. Ram the soil firmly at intervals as you proceed, particularly under shelves or around punched-out areas. Also test periodically that the pool edges remain absolutely level. Finally, fill the container with water. It should be ready for planting if it is a pool with an attached artificial rock or paved edge. A plain-edged pool, on the other hand, sunk to its rim in the soil, will have to be given a border of rocks, turf or paving before it is planted, otherwise debris may fall inside. In these cases it is better to delay filling until all the construction work is finished. When paving stones or rocks are used, they should project slightly over the pool edge, so that they disguise the nature of the pool and the fact that it is artificial.

The installation of an average-sized fibreglass pool is not difficult, as long as you approach the task methodically:
1 After marking out the site, dig down to the level of the first shelf of the mould. Use a spirit level to make sure that the site is level.
2 Allow about 2.5cm (1in) for the bedding sand, mark out the width of the shelf, then excavate down to the next level. Repeat this until the profile matches the mould. Try the pool form for size and fit and check that it is level.
3 When the pool fits neatly on the bedding sand, fill it with water. Check for any leaks and backfill the edges with soil. The rim of the pool should be level with the patio (or lawn).
4 An edging of concrete, with plants and shrubs completes the pool. Alternatively, it could be edged with turf or paving stones.

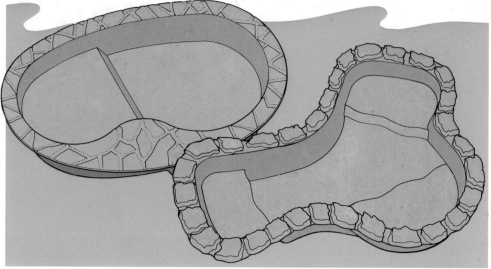

Above *Plastic sheeting, plain or reinforced, is available in various grades and for different purposes. Make sure that you buy the correct type if you want it as a pool liner. The best material is PVC but a double thickness of 500 gauge sheeting will also be strong enough for smaller pools.*

Above right *Rigid, pre-moulded liners are relatively expensive but strong and long-lasting. They have in-built ledges to accommodate plants, though this means that a hole has to be dug to match the profile.*

Fibreglass pools are available in several colours, notably pearl grey, buff, sandstone brown and sky blue. If you want the pond to look natural, choose a dark shade. Blue will remain blue in a swimming pool which is constantly being emptied and cleaned, but has little point in a garden pool open to drifting leaves and other debris, or in one containing soil that is constantly being stirred up by fish.

The advantages of fibreglass pools include their lightness, for most can be carried by a child or on the roof-rack of a car. They are quickly and easily installed, there are no problems concerning chemicals seeping from them as is the case with new concrete, so that they can be planted and stocked immediately after installation and can be taken up and moved if necessary at very short notice.

Disadvantages lie in a certain sameness about the designs and their limited size. They are also rather expensive. The flimsier vacuum-formed, semi-rigid plastic types are not worth moving, being prone to distortion and easily damaged, especially when they have been in the ground for some time.

Pool liners

At its simplest, a pool liner is a flexible sheet used to give a hole in the ground a water-proof lining. The first liners were made of thick polythene sheeting (500 or 1000 gauge) but it was soon discovered that these could be easily vandalized, as well as

damaged by a garden fork or sharp stones under the sheeting. Nowadays much stronger materials are used and most liners are either made from butyl rubber or polyvinyl chloride, commonly called PVC. When PVC in turn is reinforced with nylon it becomes exceptionally strong and stretchy, so that in spite of its flimsy appearance it is able to fit over any bumps or unevenness at the base of a pool, regardless of shape or size. Butyl is also long-lasting and strong, and for many years has been used all over the world in the construction of reservoirs. It has an estimated life in excess of 50 years and, if required, can be made larger by vulcanizing on extra sections.

A flexible liner is almost as easy to install in order to make a pool as a prefabricated fibreglass shell. Metre for metre, it is also much less expensive, and another advantage is that you are not governed by the size of a ready-made receptacle. There are no limita-tions in the case of liners. Construction is simple, planting can take place immediately this is completed and, if you tire of your pool, it can be emptied and the liner lifted and washed, then packed away until needed.

Calculating the size

Before purchasing a pool liner a rough guide as to the size you will require can be arrived at by calculating as follows: add the length of the pool to twice the maximum depth (dis-regarding any pockets or marginal shelves). Add the maximum width to twice the maximum depth.

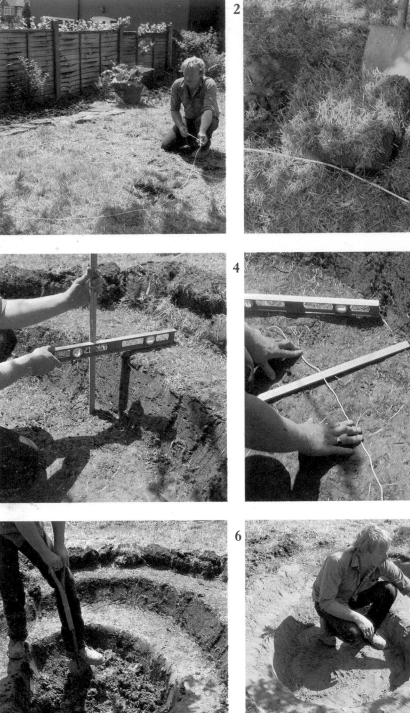

Preparing the excavation for a pool liner is quite easy. Remember, however, that the sides should be sloped to an angle of 60° or they will cave in. This means that, for a deep pool, all other dimensions must be correspondingly large.

1 *Having selected the site, mark out the shape of the pool using a length of string.*

2 *Remove the turves and stack them on one side. They can be used for edging the finished pool or for repairing other areas of lawn.*

3 *Excavate down to the depth of the first shelf. Use a spirit level and depth stick to make sure that the base is flat and even and that the slope is correctly angled.*

4 *On the flat base of the excavation, mark the outline of the shelf using a length of string to ensure the width is consistent.*

5 *Excavate down to the depth of the second shelf. Again, check that the base is level and even and that the slope is correctly angled.*

6 *Remove any stones or sharp objects from the hole and spread a layer of sand across the entire area to a depth of 2.5cm (1in).*

Thus a pool 2.4m (8ft) long × 1.8m (6ft) wide × 45cm (18in) deep would require a liner 3.3 × 2.7m (11 × 9ft). There is no need to calculate for overlap as the material usually stretches enough to allow for this, but as a double check tell the aquatic dealer the measurement of your pool before purchase.

Installation
To install a pool liner, the soil has first to be excavated – after the outline has been marked out with a length of rope, as suggested for concrete pools. There is no need to stick to a uniform depth; instead it is desirable to have several levels. Thus the main section should be 45–60cm (18–24in) deep to take care of the fish, oxygenators and water-lilies, with a shelf, or possibly shelves, only 20cm (8in) deep to take the marginal aquatics.

If the intention is to have a paved edging,

With the excavation complete you can now fit the liner:
1 *Unfold the liner and spread it evenly across the excavation. Weight the edges down with bricks. This will keep the liner in place when it is filled with water.*
2 *Run water into the pool and allow the liner to stretch into place. Move the bricks as necessary so that the weight of the water can push the liner into the profile of the hole. When full, pleat the liner around the edges and cut off the surplus to leave at least 15cm (6in) overlap.*
3 *The finished pool can be edged with turf or with paving slabs bedded on a mortar mix. The slabs should jut out over the edge of the pool by about 5cm (2in). Set the stones level with or just below the grass surround.*

1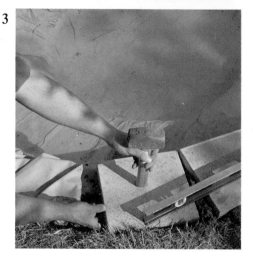

2

3

flush with a turf or soil surround, it would be a good idea to remove about 5cm (2in) of extra soil, the thickness of the paving stones, at the same time as you excavate for the pool. This saves disturbing the site once the pool is finished.

Back at the main excavation, remove any sharp stones or tree roots from the bottom and sides and tamp the soil down firmly if it is of a crumbly nature. Next spread 2.5cm (1in) of damp sand, sifted soil, ashes or even a good layer of newspapers over the base.

Drape the pool liner over the hole, leaving an even overlap of 30cm (12in) or so on all sides and secure the edges from slipping inside by anchoring them down with bricks or heavy stones. The liner can sag a little but should not be tucked down or wrinkles will form. Now run in water from a hose and, as the weight builds up, the liner will stretch and sink down to fit neatly around the shelves and bottom.

With a very large pool it is advisable to ease the strain on the material caused by a gradually increasing weight of water, by removing a few of the anchoring bricks from time to time. The liner will ease its way downwards and, when the pond is completely full of water, remove the rest of the

anchors and check for level. Adjust any faults in this direction by packing soil under the rims, then take scissors and cut away all excess liner material apart from about 15cm (6in) all round the sides. This surplus should be hidden out of sight under paving stones, rocks, turf or even soil and plants, according to whether the pool is formal or informal.

Butyl rubber or PVC sheeting can also be used to line such features as simulated streams, cascades or waterfalls, but these are difficult to make watertight. When using such accessories, it is better to install some of the fibreglass units sold by water garden specialists. Prefabricated large and small waterfalls, cascades and streamlets are all available in this material and can be linked to any type of artificial pool including concrete or flexible liners.

Ideas for small pools

Any watertight container which has nothing toxic in its makeup can usually be used for water plants and fish. Small receptacles are particularly useful where weight is a problem, as for example on balconies or roof gardens, but they can also fit in with existing garden features. There are often places in rock gardens, for instance, where small containers are useful for housing special plants, such as pygmy water-lilies or double kingcups, even by those who do not have a proper water garden. With several containers it is also possible to keep varieties of plants and fish separate; an important consideration for a keen fish breeder trying to protect timid or slow-moving ornamental kinds from attack by aggressive neighbours, such as catfish or sticklebacks.

Obvious containers include throwouts from the house like old baths, deep sinks, storage tanks and coppers. The first are fine for the purpose and when sunk to their rims in the ground and planted at the outside edges with trailing plants can be

Tubs and wooden containers can be used on their own or incorporated in a more adventurous design in which the pool construction itself adds to the interest.

quite attractive. Creeping Jenny *(Lysimachia nummularia)* is particularly suitable for this purpose as it will creep from soil to water and seems equally at home in both. A bath is roomy enough to take a water-lily, half a dozen oxygenators, two or three emergent shallow-water aquatics and four to six fish. After sinking the bath and testing it for levels, spread 10–12.5cm (4–5in) of heavy soil over the bottom, plant the water-lily and topdress the soil with clean, washed shingle. Fill the bath with water, add the oxygenators, also the marginal aquatics, which should be in pots, and prop the latter up on bricks so that their crowns are just covered with water. The fish can go in about five days later.

Lead containers are few and far between today and, although you can use them for aquatics, they are not suitable for fish. One must be wary, too, of copper, although this is alright for aquatic plants. Zinc tanks can be sunk into the soil and planted as for baths. If in doubt about toxicity, you can line containers with polythene sheeting, as this will form a barrier between the water and metal.

Other good containers are wooden tubs, sawn down to about 50cm (20in). Those which have held beer, wine or vinegar are best. Soap and oily substances are difficult to remove but this can be done by stuffing the tubs with dry hay or straw and setting light to it. The fire must not be allowed to burn too long, only enough to lightly char the inside. When this stage is reached, turn the tub upside down so that the flames are smothered.

All tubs should be scrubbed and well rinsed before use, also kept full of water for several days – replenished as necessary – if they leak. This will cause the staves to swell and render the tub watertight. Plant as suggested for baths, with soil at the bottom, picking a small variety of water-lily such as any of the 'Odorata' or 'Laydekeri' hybrids. Tubs can either be sunk into the ground or used free standing. One idea is to sink several close together in a depression, keeping a separate variety of water-lily and possibly a distinct kind of fish in each. Plant a few bog plants between the tubs and regularly flood these over so that the soil around becomes boggy.

Garden centres sometimes sell large concrete or plastic urns and containers for growing shrubs and trees in offices. If these have drainage holes they can be lined with polythene, otherwise there is no need, and used to make mini-pools. The lightweight plastic containers are excellent for roof gardens and all can be attractive in patios.

CHAPTER 3
OPTIONAL EXTRAS

A pool will prove an attractive feature in its own right but there are various accessories to broaden its appeal: fountains, waterfalls and many lighting effects are just some of the choices open to you.

Many people are happy to settle for a simple, natural-looking pool (assuming of course that the pool was not natural in the first place) and have no wish to embellish it with fountains, waterfalls, floodlighting or underwater lighting. They are content to see the reflection of the clouds in the pool and to watch the leisurely progress of the fish. True, the pool has to be fairly large to be of much interest in the latter respect and formal pools both large and small can be made much more interesting with fountains, tumbling water and lighting. Fortunately, modern equipment has made the installation of these kind of features much easier than in the past.

Waterfalls and fountains
Waterfalls are only appropriate in water gardens of a natural kind. Similarly, fountains are inappropriate for informal pools which have simulated streams tumbling down over rocks or any with artificial plastic 'rock' courses. However, fountains can make splendid embellishments to a formal pool and have many variations as regards spray patterns. An additional attraction is provided by colourful lighting.

Waterfalls
Few people have a natural slope in their garden down which they can construct a water channel that will send water cascading into a pool. But, if soil has been excavated to make the pool and this forms part of a combined rock and water garden, then, by using the soil to build up height at the back, it is quite possible to form a gentle slope down which water can tumble.

Whatever the decision and whether you aim to make your own concrete water course or buy plastic or fibreglass units, you need to have a small 'collection area' – a shallow basin at the top into which the water is supplied to start the flow and from which it can run down via the channel and into the pool.

As with the making of pools, plastic or fibreglass water courses are easier to install than concrete and will not crack with age or split if water freezes in them in winter.

When laying a stream channel, whether it is of concrete or prefabricated units, the tricky part comes when the water falls from one level to another lower down, or finally into the pool. It should be remembered that water never falls in a perfectly straight line or even flow – instead it follows the line of least resistance through softer areas of soil or rock and so flows irregularly from one side to another. You only have to walk along a river bank for evidence of this fact.

Accordingly, you should try to emulate this natural flow pattern by providing obstacles, such as setting pieces of stone to divert the flow from a straight downward course. For such small channels prefabricated plastic fibreglass or concrete water courses are suitable and they will be waterproof and easy to install. Alternatively, anyone of a DIY bent could make a firm base to the water course by ramming broken rubble in the bottom and then laying a concrete channel – shaped to the required depth – on top of this.

In a man-made waterfall, water is normally conducted to the top of the fall through a plastic pipe. This should be hidden 2.5cm (1in) or so under soil, and will connect in turn to the outflow from an electric pump. The functions and installation of electric pumps that supply water to waterfalls and fountains are explained later in this chapter.

Fountains
There are many types and patterns available in fountains so it is worthwhile taking the trouble to examine and find out something about them before making your choice. Some will probably be more suitable than others for your particular pool. For example, there are more than a dozen jet patterns available in various types of fountain – from single jets, to two, three or even four tier jets. There is the so-called "mushroom" or water-tulip kind which throws a bell-shaped jet of water, as well as a fountain that produces three bell-shaped jets. Another kind produces a foaming jet – an effect obtained by mixing air with water.

Whether simple or ornate, a fountain will give a distinctive touch to the smallest pool and the ever-changing patterns and sounds of moving water will bring special pleasure during the long, hot days of summer.

If you want a waterfall in the garden, you can choose between a ready moulded unit or your own construction. Either way, it is important to begin by working out a design on paper: the most effective will have a collection pool at the top, with a cascade leading down to a second pool. Home-made water courses can be tricky to construct, but the pre-moulded units come in a variety of combinations and are very easy to install.

1 Mark out the site with pegs and string, then arrange the components roughly in place.

2 If starting on level ground, build up the soil base to the required height. Work from the lowest point upwards, compact the soil with the back of a spade and check that the bases are level when the components are in place.

3 Add about 12mm (½in) builder's sand to provide a smooth bedding surface. Lay the mouldings in place, again checking that the bases are level. Fill the pools with water and backfill with sand or sifted soil. Pack it in hard, especially around the shelves. These will sag and disrupt the flow of water if not properly supported.

4 Run the hose to the top of the course and cover it with rocks and soil.

One elaborate fountain displays a series of automatically changing patterns, producing 18 patterns in a set sequence with each spray pattern continuing for 12 to 16 seconds. The complete sequence lasts about 3½ minutes. Depending on the power of the pump providing the pressure, the spray height achieved with this fountain can be 2.1m (7ft) or so, covering a circle with a diameter of 1.3m (4½ft) or more.

Some fountains are illuminated from below, which provides charming rainbow effects, particularly at night. The lamp is situated immediately underneath the fountain jet and water passes over and around the coloured lens of this lamp before entering the jet.

In addition to the wide range of simple single or multiple jet fountains, which are designed to operate from the surface level of the pool, there are hosts of ornamental fountains and spouting ornaments designed to eject water. This is usually through the mouth, for example by a frog sitting on a toadstool or the ever-popular designs of statues and figurines.

Another attractive idea is to install a raised large circular stone basin with a fountain unit in its centre. Water produced by this will then splash over the sides into another basin lower down or alternatively into the pool. Some models have three tiers of basins and make attractive centre-pieces for small formal pools.

Installation of pumps

For a system of waterfalls and fountains the pump, of course, is the paramount component. Pumps come in various sizes and at widely differing prices according to the type of electric motor involved and the general quality of the materials and workmanship. You get what you pay for, as with most bits of modern equipment. Before deciding which type and pump size to buy you must determine what you want it to do. Thus, decide whether it is to provide the power to operate one or more fountains, or just one waterfall, or perhaps a waterfall and a fountain.

Another point to consider is whether you wish now or at some future date to install garden lighting, either on the surface or under the water. All these factors have to be borne in mind when deciding the size of the pump to be installed, as well as the switch gear and other items involved, if a fairly ambitious set-up is envisaged.

There are two types of electric pump: the submersible pumps which are placed under water in the pool and surface pumps which have to be installed in a waterproof building indoors – in a shed or garage or in a specially built pump-house. Then there is a further division, in that there are mains voltage pumps and also low voltage pumps which are operated from a transformer. In the event of fairly long distances occurring between the source of the mains supply and

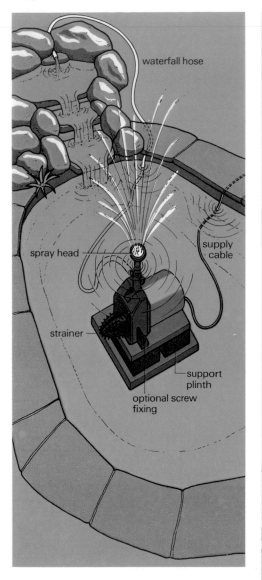

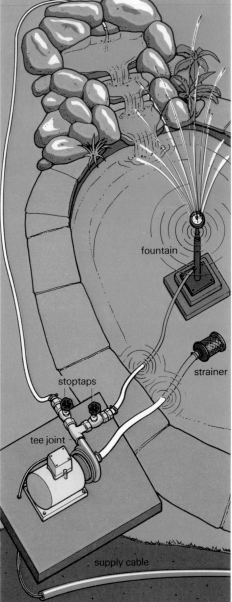

Far left *Submersible pumps are the easiest kind to install. They are fully waterproofed and need simply to be placed in the pool with the waterproof cable running to a connection with an outdoor electrical supply. Some are powerful enough to drive both a waterfall and fountain, though the pump output will determine the height and size of these. The water is sucked in through a strainer and pumped to the fountain and/or the head of the waterfall.*

Left *Surface pumps generally have a longer working life and greater output than the submersible types. They must be housed in a waterproof chamber (not shown). Hoses feed the fountain and/or waterfall in the same way as a submersible pump, but the water is sucked in through a remote strainer in the pool connected to the inlet side of the pump.*

the various installations then a mains voltage pump is essential.

The scope of low voltage transformers is limited because of the drop in voltage which occurs if there is a considerable length of cable from the transformer to the pump, fountain or lighting equipment. The range of cable length from the low voltage output side of a transformer should not be much more than about 7–9m (23–30ft). When the cable is more than about 12m (40ft) long there will usually be a voltage drop which means a reduction in the performance of the pump or fountain.

In small gardens, however, a low voltage system has much to commend it, as it is quite safe and if, as will be seen later, portable lights are to be used, a low voltage supply is really the only sensible choice.

There are also two different types of pump. The older, series-wound pumps with carbon 'brushes', wear out and require frequent renewal. These are not recommended for continuous use. Those with an induction motor are of modern design and sophisticated materials capable of continuous running to provide water for a waterfall or fountain. The latter are the best to buy.

There is yet one more choice to be made, between the surface or the submersible pump. For all but the largest installations in gardens, the submersible pumps are the more popular choice. They usually come fitted with a strainer, a priming valve and a sufficient length of cable to connect to a waterproof plug and socket on the cable leading from the mains supply. The beauty of these submersible pumps is that there is virtually no plumbing necessary; a hose is connected to the fountain and, if desired, a waterfall, and the pump is just placed in the pool at the recommended depth below the surface, set on a base of bricks or something similar. The water is then pumped up from the pool, recirculated and sent back to the pool again. For further information on the electrical installation and safety considerations see page 29.

The range and performance of these submersible pumps is quite remarkable, from the simplest, relatively inexpensive, types, delivering an output of 910 L (200 gal) an hour with a lift of 1m (3ft), to the larger, more expensive models, delivering 1500 L (330 gal) an hour or more.

The right approach to the problem of choosing a pump for your water garden is to measure the height above ground level of the topmost water course. Then decide whether you wish to supply water only to the waterfalls, to a fountain only, or both, or, in the case of larger installations, if you wish to supply a waterfall and perhaps several fountains. Armed with this information you can go to a garden centre where, hopefully, you will be able to obtain advice on the size of pump, the choice of fountains and receive good counsel about the installation of all this equipment.

When you have to take a mains voltage supply from the source in the house it should be by means of an armoured cable if it is to be buried in the soil. This should be buried at least 60cm (24in) deep and preferably covered with concrete tiles, if there is any danger that the cable might be disturbed by somebody digging the ground above it.

All cables carrying mains voltage should be protected by what used to be called an 'earth leakage trip switch' but is now called a 'residual current device or current breaker' (RCD or RCCB). One can fit a flush fitting 13 amp socket RCD combination. Or there is a separate plug incorporating the RCD which is fitted with a test button which will show immediately if there is any fault on the line. If this unit 'trips' – if a fault develops – it must be removed from the socket. It cannot be reset until the fault is rectified. These circuit breakers should be used whenever mains voltage cables are taken outdoors for any purpose – to supply pumps, fountains, lighting, pool heaters and, of course, all kinds of electrical equipment such as lawn mowers, scarifiers, hedge trimmers, power tools such as electric drills – in fact, any appliance whose attendant cable could possibly be cut or become frayed in use.

Electricity and the water garden

Installing mains voltage wiring in the garden is no field of endeavour for the home handyman. It should always be carried out or checked by a qualified electrician – even in the home, let alone in the garden where danger of a possibly fatal electric shock is so much greater. You should make sure that the firm employed to do such work is on the roll of the National Inspection Council for Electrical Installation Contracting. Your local electricity board and any contractor on the above roll will willingly give expert help on problems of

Installing a submersible pump is a straightforward task that need only take a few minutes:
1 Assemble the components and check that none is mising. Assemble according to the manufacturer's instructions.
2 Measure the height of the spray head. You may have to build an underwater plinth to bring the spray to the required height. It should be just above the surface of the water.
3 After building the plinth, install the pump in position (you may have to secure it to the plinth by using a wooden block). If you have a waterfall, feed the hose to the top collection pool, avoiding any sharp bends or twists. Cut the hose to length and wedge the end firmly in place between two or three rocks. The pump is now ready for connection to the power source.

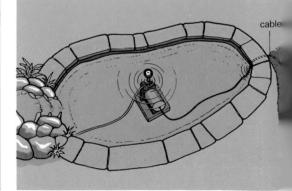

outdoor electrical wiring. A leaflet 'Safety in the Garden' is available from your local electricity showroom.

There are stringent regulations governing the type of cable, switches, light sockets, as well as the junction boxes, actual laying of cable or fixing it to walls. Fixing to fences is not permitted. Such installations must be adequately earthed. It is also desirable that a residual current device – an RCD – is installed to provide additional safety.

Extensions from, say, a power socket in the house are not considered safe enough for taking cable carrying mains voltage out to the garden to operate pumps, fountains or pool lighting. All such installations should have a separate main switch and be separately fused. A much safer way of using electricity in the garden is to install a transformer, either in the house or garage, or some other waterproof building. These transformers provide low voltage current, usually 12 volts, which is safe to use in the garden.

Garden lighting equipment that can be attached to the outside wall of the house may be connected to the normal domestic installation but these types of lamp and any other equipment must be waterproof and approved for outdoor use. There are specialist firms who deal in all aspects of water gardens, pools and the like and, of course, offer a wide choice of equipment. It would pay to consult an electrician about the best type of equipment to buy and then shop around to see what it will cost.

Left *Outdoor lighting will enable you to enjoy your garden long after the sun goes down and its artificial effects can be used to set a mood of mystery, adventure or light-hearted festivity.*

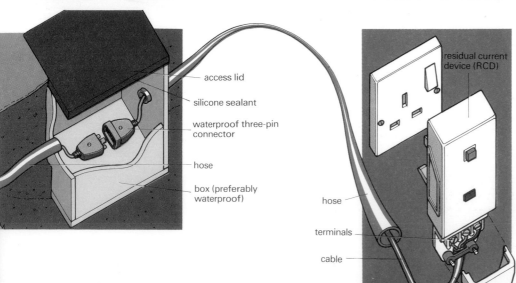

access lid

silicone sealant

waterproof three-pin connector

hose

box (preferably waterproof)

residual current device (RCD)

hose

terminals

cable

Below left *For a mains electrical connection, the submersible pump cable should be buried in a trench and sheathed with hose-pipe for added protection (use plastic conduit for surface mounting). House the cable connector in a waterproof box fitted with a removable lid. Make sure that the pins of the connector are on the pump side. At the supply end, fit an RCCB (residual current contact breaker) rather than an ordinary plug.*

For maximum visual effect, why not install pool lighting so that the sprays of a fountain can be seen shimmering in the night? Even more dramatic is the impact of underwater lighting, where different colours can be used singly or in groups.

Garden lighting

Garden lighting can take many forms. The simplest is probably several 500 watt lamps fixed to an outside wall which will illuminate the whole area around the house at the touch of a switch indoors. Apart from their value in lighting up the garden and for evening barbecue parties, outdoor lamps are also useful as burglar deterrents – if you hear strange sounds after dark, you can switch on the lights and few intruders would be fool enough to press on with any invasion of your property. As an added precaution, it would obviously be desirable to have another switch upstairs as well as one downstairs. Other outdoor floodlighting installations can also be connected to an indoor switch for the same deterrent purpose.

There is a wide range of lighting equipment available for use in gardens and on patios. Large weatherproof 200 watt or 100 watt lamps are available for mounting on walls or trees or on a spike which is then pushed into the ground. These are obviously ideal for spotlighting part of a building or a tree as well as the pool.

Perhaps even more interesting are the sets of portable low voltage lights which work from a transformer. You can fit up to ten 25 watt lamps, using this method. They can be stuck into the ground on short spikes. The lamps may be placed to illuminate awkward corners or hazards such as steps in the garden or to highlight some particular garden feature. You can, for example, place one of these lamps to light up a flowering cherry tree and then move it on to illuminate a playing waterfall or, in due course, some other garden feature. Certain of these sets have interchangeable clear or coloured lenses and it is remarkable how, for example, a red lens greatly enhances the beauty of a red flowered tree, shrub or group of herbaceous plants. Naturally the same effect is produced with coloured lenses directed towards blue or yellow flowered plants.

Now to perhaps the most exciting outdoor lighting of all – underwater lighting in pools or to illuminate fountains. There are both mains voltage lamps with up to 150 watt capacity, capable of producing very powerful lighting to illuminate fountains, and low voltage submersible lamps working from a transformer which can float on a pool or be set to illuminate a fountain or a waterfall.

All modern underwater lighting equipment is doubly insulated, in the case of mains voltage lamps, and with low voltage lights, they are waterproof.

As with pump installations, any lighting equipment, unless it is fixed permanently to a wall, should be protected by an RCD – a circuit breaker – which will cut off the current if a fault should develop in the outside wiring system or if a cable should be accidently cut.

Pool surrounds

Formal pools call for formal surrounds and these may be of various materials. York paving is not recommended, though it is sometimes obtainable at quite reasonable prices from local authorities, because it can become very slippery should it become coated with even a very thin layer of green algae. Nowadays there are excellent paving slabs in various sizes, easy to lay and not slippery. They are made to resemble sandstone paving but, if a bright modern look is desired, there are also coloured paving slabs available. Variety may be provided by inserting occasionally between the slabs a square filled with cobble stones set in concrete, or, if a quantity of old tiles is available, a square of these set edgeways in concrete will also break up the monotony of an area of plain paving. Again, a combination of red bricks and plain sand coloured paving can be very pleasing but try to seek out well-fired, wire-cut bricks. These, unlike ordinary bricks, are less likely to become slippery in frosty weather and do not seem to be so much affected by algae.

Whether or not the pool is built to be partly above ground, it is still possible to build a low wall around a formal pool, with or without a flat stone capping. The latter is handy to sit on or makes somewhere to set down a teacup or tumbler as you recline in a deckchair beside the pool.

For a less formal appearance, you can

The finishing touches to this pool have helped make it a favourite corner of the garden. The formal surrounds, appropriate to the formal design, are softened by low-growing plants, while a small statue, framed by flowers, creates a quiet arbour at the side.

An irregularly-shaped pool looks especially effective when edged with crazy paving.

use broken, or 'crazy', paving and there is much to be said for this type of surround if spaces are left here and there into which may be planted low-growing plants, such as thymes, thrifts, aubrietas, dwarf campanulas, helianthemums and the like. This type of surround usually looks better when built in conjunction with an irregularly shaped pool rather than a square, rectangular or circular one, although it has a place with any shape of pool if some degree of informality is desired (as when a pool is set in an area of lawn). Surrounds to pools which have a rocky finish, or with rock or simulated rock waterfalls, look best if grass is brought up to the water's edge or if a boggy area is provided.

Another effective treatment for a pool set in grass is to have a very small paved area around and approached by stepping stones set in the turf. These should be set slightly lower than the turf so that the mower can ride over them without damage to the blades. You should also try to lay the stones so that they approach the pool from several different directions, so that visitors can go and admire it, and then proceed on a tour of the garden without having to retrace their steps. Stepping stones and, indeed, all paths should always lead to somewhere interesting – or at least give promise that they will do so. Paths should never finish abruptly or at a fence with no possibility of going on.

Problem-saving accessories

Pools also bring problems. If made of concrete they will almost certainly, in time,

begin to leak. A more common problem is that of algae fouling the water and making it impossible to see the fish. Even when a balance has been achieved in the relationship of fish and oxygenating plants, it can happen that further action has to be taken to keep water free from certain types of unsightly algae.

Pools freeze in winter and fish may die. Leaves may fall into the pond and lie on the bottom to rot, giving off noxious gases which may be harmful to the fish, especially if the pool freezes over and there is no provision made to keep a small area free from ice.

Leaking pools

Leaks in concrete can hopefully be prevented if the pool is well made with the sides and bottom at least 15cm (6in) thick, and later the surface is treated with a sealing primer to neutralise any free lime, and then followed by a powerful pondseal. This takes the form of a plastic paint and is available from water plant specialists in blue or natural stone colour. Such compounds may be applied to give an attractive and waterproof finish to new pools, or to repair porous, leaky or cracked pools, in spring after any danger of frost is past. There are various brands and kinds of sealants, all of which must be applied according to the manufacturers' instructions. Normally they are not applied in winter or when the air temperature is below 10°C (50°F).

Aquatic dealers also stock waterproofing powders which can be added to concrete mixes to increase the water-holding capacity of the mix.

Dealing with algae

One of the most worrying and persistent problems with pools is that caused by green algae, including the type called blanket weed. These make the water cloudy or unsightly.

In small pools, if the balance of fish and oxygenating plants is right, the water will clear after an initial greening period and remain clear. But in larger pools where perhaps the balance between fish and plants has not been achieved, the water may remain green and murky. This is more fully described on page 39. Every attempt should be made to clear the water by natural means, such as using plenty of underwater vegetation and balancing the quota of fish and plants.

Because the quantity of water in an artificial garden pool is of necessity limited, introducing chemical controls for algae can be tricky. It takes very little to overdo the dose with dire results, particularly for fish.

However, there are people who claim success from using algicides and there are several preparations on the market which have been formulated to control blanket weed and green water and which, it is claimed, will not harm plants or fish. If you use any of these do adhere strictly to the recommended quantities, but, more importantly, try to plant the pool correctly initially.

Biological filters

More recently, biological filters have come on the market. These are designed to operate outside the pool and they work continuously during spring, summer and autumn but are not necessarily active in winter. Their purpose is to break down and purify – with the aid of beneficial bacteria – solids derived from fish excreta, dead snails, algae and plants and turn them into harmless material capable of being absorbed as food by plants.

The filter is sited outside the pond, suitably camouflaged at the top of a waterfall where water is pumped through, brought up from the pool farther down and then returned to it again via the waterfall. Alternatively, the filter can be hidden somewhere near a static pool, a pump constantly sending water from the latter through the filter and back again to the pool. Quite small pumps are suitable for these filters but since they must run continuously, a submersible type is recommended. The water passes over a special gravel or foam medium on which beneficial bacteria form, converting waste materials into plant foods. It takes four to six weeks for the full effect of this biological filtration to become fully effective, after which the only servicing consists of occasional cleaning of the filter foam.

Pool heaters

Ice forming on pools in winter presents another problem, particularly for fish. Methods of dealing with this hazard in the case of small pools is described on page 40 but, if you do not want the bother of these, you can keep an area clear with an electric pond heater. These consist of a 125 watt heating element enclosed in a rod type tube, which in turn is suspended from a block of polystyrene. This keeps it floating and upright in the water and will, when in use, keep an area of about 2.8 sq m (30 sq ft) clear of ice. The heater may be connected to a mains voltage supply in the house but, as with all other appliances used outdoors should be protected by an RCD.

Nets and netting

Other accessories obtainable from aquatic specialists include fish nets of various sizes.

The small ones are useful for catching the odd fish, perhaps ill or injured, and removing it to other quarters; the larger kinds for removing floating debris or leaves as well as catching fish. There is even a net sold with an amazing 2.3m (7½ft) telescopic handle.

A number of firms sell pool nets, made of plastic with 10–20mm (⅜–¾in) mesh. Sizes vary from 3 × 2m (10 × 6½ft) up to 10.9 × 3.6m (36 × 12ft). Stretched over a pool and pegged at the edges they can be used to trap leaves or submerged below the water surface to deter herons and gulls from stealing the fish.

Herons, incidentally, do not fly or jump into a pond, but walk in from the edge and, when their feet become entangled in the net, they admit defeat and turn their attentions elsewhere.

Herons, apparently, are fiercely jealous of their particular territories and nowadays you can buy very life-like plastic models of herons which, if placed near pools, streams or even on river banks, will deter live herons from invading the garden.

Cats can also be a nuisance, snatching up fish from a pool. If there are cats around causing problems, it would pay you well to stretch a small meshed net right over the top of the pool.

For contending with cold winters and the problem of ice forming on pools, one solution is to use a pond heater.

CHAPTER 4
MANAGEMENT & MAINTENANCE

When your pool is complete, one of the most enjoyable tasks can be tackled – choosing from the many different water plants. There are also a number of routine checks you should make, however, to keep the pool in good order.

As soon as a pool is constructed it is natural to want to see it planted. But, before attempting to install any plants or fish, it is wise to check that the pool – or pools if there is more than one – are watertight and sit level in the soil. Since this probably represents the last opportunity to correct any unevenness or irregularities, it is worth spending a little time checking.

Also, if the pool is constructed of concrete, it will be necessary to mature the inside before plants are introduced. Most aquatics favour slightly acid rather than alkaline conditions, but the cement in new concrete releases lime into the water. This does not persist forever, but does continue to seep out for some time and, when it occurs, some plants will unaccountably fail. The effect on fish, however, will be more dramatic, because lime causes their fins to split and fray – and in some cases it kills.

For these reasons, people in the past usually made concrete pools in the autumn. They were then kept full of water all winter. Apart from giving them a good test against leakage, this period allowed most of the free lime to escape into the water. When the pool was emptied in spring, all harmful material was removed, and it was possible to plant with safety.

In the case of a late construction, however, acid was sometimes added to a filled pool in an attempt to neutralize its alkalinity. The commonest kind used was commercial syrupy phosphoric acid, added in sufficient quantity to show an acid reaction to litmus paper twice in twenty-four hours. Fortunately, today there are sealing compounds which make neither a long wait nor such chemical treatment necessary. This sealing agent is painted over the whole of the concrete interior where it blocks off any pollution. Sometimes the sealer is combined with a waterproofing agent.

Of course, none of this preliminary treatment is needed for prefabricated or polythene lined ponds. These can be planted as soon as convenient after they are constructed.

Planting water-lilies

Water-lilies, with their large, tuberous roots are the most expensive aquatic plants you are likely to buy and also those which most resent disturbance. Some kinds take a long time to get over a move, especially if they are initially put into very deep water. For this reason they should always be moved in spring, before growth is very far advanced but the sap is rising, so that new roots are quickly produced.

The roots of hardy water-lilies take two forms. Some have their tubers running horizontally through the soil like the rhizome of a bearded iris, while others are more upright and grow after the fashion of a carrot. Another interesting fact is that most of the fragrant water-lilies have horizontal tubers – the species and cultivars of *Nymphaea odorata* and *N. tuberosa*, for example.

To plant water-lilies, you must either establish them in soil already covering the base of the pool or plant them in baskets. For the first method it is usual to drain off the water, or plant them in the soil before water is added. This is certainly a practical method with very small containers, for example tubs, baths or tiny rock pools. In such cases there should be about 12.5cm (5in) of soil over the base and, after planting the lilies with a trowel, a top dressing of shingle should be spread on the surface and the water run in carefully to avoid disturbing soil or plants. If the hose is run into a flower pot lying on its side this is enough to slow the force of most jets.

This is not a suitable method for a large expanse of water, like a lake. In cases like this, the lily roots must be weighted and lowered in position, so that they can root into the muddy soil below at their own pace. This can be achieved either by planting

The choice of plants to go in and around a pool is almost infinite and, once established, they will require only occasional checks to ensure that they are healthy. In this woodland setting, interest comes as much from the surrounding foliage as the pool itself and, in the foreground, the cool colours of Hydrangea paniculata *complement the mood perfectly.*

Water-lilies are best planted in baskets placed in the appropriate depth of water for the particular variety (see page 54).
1 Assemble the materials: a basket, compost, plastic-coated wire and sacking, plus the water-lily.
2 Line the basket with sacking and fill the base with compost.
3 Bed the crown of the water-lily well into the compost.
4 Pack added compost around the plant, making it as secure as possible.
5 Wrap sacking around to form a neat 'parcel' that will prevent compost from spilling out.
6 Tie the parcel firmly before the basket is sunk in water.

1
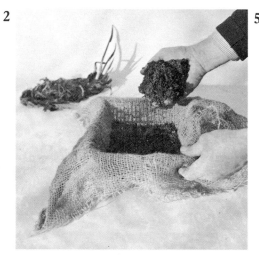

2
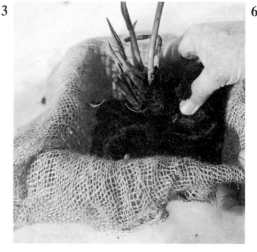

3

4

5

6

them in baskets first, preferably of wicker or cane as this will eventually rot away or, alternatively, sandwich each root between two turves turned grass-side inwards. The grass should be shaved very short beforehand and the packages tied together with tape, which is less likely to cut through the bundles than string. The water-lilies should then be carefully lowered, so that they settle the right way up.

Undoubtedly, however, the easiest and most satisfactory method of growing water-

lilies today is to plant them in the aquatic baskets obtainable from dealers. These are made of plastic and have perforations round the sides for, curiously, the roots like to feel the influence of water and should not be forced into solid containers. Baskets are not only economical of soil but can be quickly lowered into place and, if necessary, lifted and replanted easily and without fuss.

The compost used for water-lilies should be on the heavy side, such as good garden soil or turf which has rotted down over a long period, so that there is no longer any evidence of roots or fibrous shoots. This can either be mixed with ⅙th of its bulk well-rotted cow manure or, if this is difficult to come by, with coarse bone-meal, used at the rate of a handful per basket. Because there may be a slight risk of contracting anthrax from bone-meal, always wear gloves when handling this substance.

Plant each water-lily firmly in its basket, up to the old planting mark and to within 4cm (1½in) of the top. Dampening the compost beforehand enables it to be packed down fairly easily. Next, top-dress the baskets with 2.5cm (1in) of clean washed shingle, to deter fish from rooting into the soil. Cut off any dead, damaged or broken-stemmed leaves and lower the baskets into the water. The crowns of the water-lilies should only be barely submerged at this stage, so you may have to raise the baskets on bricks for a week or two, or until new leaves can be seen coming through the soil.

If plunged under 45–60cm (18–24in) of water immediately after planting, water-lilies can be checked so badly that they may fail to flower that season, so this preliminary attention is well worthwhile.

Do not be tempted by sales talk or by well-meaning friends into adding fertilizers to water-lily compost. This applies to leafmould, compost and peat as well as chemicals. It takes very little to alter the nature of still water and the smaller the pool, the easier it is for introduced chemicals to build up to harmful proportions. You will then be faced with all the problems of decomposition and gases like methane and hydrogen sulphide occurring, plus some of the worst forms of algae. Greater liberties can be taken with a large expanse of water, such as a lake, where a wide surface area is exposed to the air.

Planting shallow-water aquatics
Most shallow-water aquatics are normally planted in pots placed on shelves or established in shallow troughs built into pools. These plants can be dealt with over a longer season than water-lilies. However, if you want to see them in flower the first season, very early bloomers like kingcups (*Caltha* spp), water forget-me-nots and giant aroids, such as lysichitons, must go in in early spring. Alternatively, wait until the flowers have gone in the case of kingcups, and deal with lysichitons when most of the foliage has died down. Most other marginal

Caltha palustris, *the marsh marigold or kingcup, is a superb plant for bog gardens and pool surrounds and its bright yellow flowers will bring a bold, attractive splash of colour to any spring-time display.*

water plants can be planted, also lifted and divided, between mid-spring and mid-summer, but even so, the earlier the better.

Plant all of these in heavy loam, without the bone-meal, as fertilizers are rarely necessary. Most aquatic plants grow rather rapidly since they do not experience the setbacks common to land plants, such as summer drought and shortage of water.

Planting oxygenators

Oxygenators rarely have many roots to worry about, but they do have to be spaced out in the pool in the first instance. To make sure that they sink to the bottom, group the slender stems together in small bunches, and either fasten these to small stones or similar weights or twist a narrow strip of lead around their bases. It is also possible to dibble a number – like cuttings – into a shallow seedtray of loam and stand this on the pool floor. Floaters present no problems as they only have to be placed on the water.

Planting bog plants

Bog plants are more individualistic, some needing richer fare than others, although the majority dislike lime. If the ground is thoroughly prepared beforehand, weeded and deeply dug with plenty of well-rotted organic material worked in, it should last a long time in fertile condition. Later, a mulch each spring of mushroom compost, leafmould, garden compost or well-rotted farmyard manure will prove beneficial for most bog plants.

Aftercare

Once your pool is filled with water, planted and occupied by fish, it should run smoothly, provided you give it reasonable maintenance and seasonal care as necessary.

Scum removal

It is not unusual for a coating of scum to appear on the water soon after planting. This is due to the newness of everything – soil, water or even something in the pool fabric. Floating debris looks unsightly and should be removed. The easiest way of doing this is to put the end of a garden hose in the pool, then turn on the water and flood it over so that the debris goes over the sides. When this is not practical, perhaps because it will swamp neighbouring land plants, pinch the end of the hose with your finger and thumb to force a strong jet and play this over the water. This breaks up any bubbles of scum and also drives the unwanted material to one end of the pool where it can be lifted out with a fish net. In the case of baths, tubs and other small containers, a quick and easy idea is to draw a sheet of newspaper across the water surface. Any scum will adhere to the paper and can then be quickly and easily removed in that way.

Should secondary crops of scum occur, try 'beating' the water surface with a powerful jet from the hose. This usually causes it to sink, and may be repeated if necessary. Whatever happens, do not make a habit of emptying and refilling your pool, as this will check growth on the part of the underwater oxygenators and also reintroduce chemicals – such as chlorine – from the fresh tap water.

Treating green water

If the water turns green this is not necessarily harmful, indeed fish may thrive in it, but admittedly it is disfiguring. The cause is due to myriads of tiny, unicellular plants called algae. These feed on dissolved salts present in the water and derive their energy from sunlight. Once the oxygenators really get going they starve the algae of food, so it is important to do everything possible to assist them in these early stages. Competition is the key to success but, if you find the greenness more than you can bear, shade the water for a day or two by laying boards or black plastic across the surface. This will stop the algae growing by denying them light, but do not keep the shading on too long or it will also adversely affect the aquatic plants.

Autumn care

As the season advances, inevitably flowers and leaves die. These should be removed on sight; those of the water-lilies by pulling them from the rootstocks. Certain aquatics, like the water plantains (Alisma) are inveterate seeders and they should have their old flower heads removed as soon as the flowers fade. Bog plants, too, should be kept neat and tidy by regular weeding and the routine removal of faded or dead vegetation.

Water-lily cultivation

When water-lilies have been in their baskets for a couple of years they will probably have exhausted most of the original food supply. To keep them going a little longer, feed them with bone-meal 'pills'. These are made by mixing together equal parts of moist clay and bone-meal and moulding the resultant 'dough' into tennis-ball sized pills. Push these pills down into the sides of the baskets, giving a large and vigorous water-lily two, but a medium-sized lily only one. After five years, at the latest, the baskets should be lifted and the water-lilies divided as necessary and replanted in fresh soil.

Opposite *Many shade-loving plants are also excellent choices for a pool-side location. Here, a raised bed features the striking foliage of* Hosta fortunei *'Albopicta', astilbes and epimedium, with a large rhubarb plant* (Rheum palmatum) *beyond. Height is provided by the delicate cut leaf sumach tree* (Rhus typhina *'Laciniata') and by a tub planted with another variegated hosta, 'Thomas Hogg'.*

Dealing with leaves

Though, ideally, pools should be sited well away from trees, this is not always possible and leaves from neighbours' trees, if not your own, may well fall into the pool in autumn. They will sink to the bottom and decompose, releasing noxious gases and salts into the water which will become harmful to fish and encourages algae. It is important to keep dredging them out with a rake or, better still, prevent the leaves getting into the pool in the first place. This is achieved by trapping them as they come tumbling down in autumn gales.

It is not too difficult to construct a light cover or screen which will fit over any small to medium-sized pool, though is out of the question for large pools where dredging is best. To make the screen, knock together a light framework of 5cm (2in) laths, a couple of inches larger all round than the area of the pond. Tack small-meshed, plastic netting between the lath edges and lay the completed cover over the pool, preferably raised on bricks to keep the netting dry. However, the bricks are not essential: the main thing is to catch the leaves before they become wet and heavy. Take the screen off – this is usually a two-person job – and empty it from time to time.

The covers should be in place by the end of early autumn and only removed for storage when all leaves are down. Incidentally, such covers are sometimes useful in spring for catching tree blossoms as well as, say, the woolly catkins from poplar trees.

Winter care

When winter finally arrives and poolside reeds and sedges become withered and brown, they should be cut down to prevent them becoming cosy winter quarters for pests. But the biggest hazard will come later with the frosts, for if these are severe and ice builds up thickly there could be danger for fish, as well as more tender plants and, possibly, concrete pools.

Where there is 45cm (18in) or more water over the water-lilies, these should come to no harm and, provided they can get air, nor will the fish. Tiny rock pools and tubs may have to be emptied and the inmates housed elsewhere for the worst of the winter or, alternatively, in milder districts, they will survive if the pool is covered with boards with sacks of straw laid on top during severe frost. Such coverings must be removed when each thaw sets in, otherwise the water-lilies may start into premature growth.

The simplest method of keeping any artificial pool that holds 45cm (18ins) or more of water from freezing up completely is to float a large ball or a block of wood on top. Do this in late autumn and then, when ice forms and is about 2.5cm (1in) thick, take a kettle of boiling water outside and pour it over the ball. When the latter loosens, take it out and bale or siphon out 2.5cm (1in) of water. Now cover the hole with a sack and leave things alone until a thaw sets in. The sack should then be removed, the pool filled again with water and the ball refloated, ready for the next frost session. The purpose of all this is to keep a hole open in the ice and to let the rest of the ice act like a sheet of glass over the unfrozen water.

It is also possible to install pool heaters in order to keep a small area of water free of ice in winter.

What can go wrong?

Although you need not anticipate much going wrong in the water garden, should troubles occur it is important to recognize and deal with them at once. This particularly applies to pests.

Construction problems

These include leaks in a concrete pool and troubles caused by free lime from new concrete polluting the water. See page 34 for ways to prevent these – before they occur. If leaks appear later and are too severe to be cured by painting over the interior, line the pool with a flexible polythene liner and start again.

Damaged liners, semi-rigid vacuum-moulded pools and prefabricated glass fibre kinds can all be repaired on site with the aid of special adhesives and patching tape. Go to a specialist aquatic firm and purchase a suitable repair kit for your type of pool. There are different kits for different kinds of pools.

Weeds

Weeds are probably the greatest nuisance in a pool as they make everything look cluttered and untidy. None is more troublesome than the green tangled masses of a particular alga called blanket weed. The main causes of rapid spread with all kinds of algae are high temperatures, bright sunlight and a superabundance of mineral salts derived from the waste products of plants and animals.

Blanket weed grows in long greenish-brown tresses which feel rough to the touch. It winds itself in a smothering embrace around the underwater parts of water-lilies and submerged plants and also clings to the pool sides. If the pool is small the best way to remove it is by hand, as it can then be disentangled from brittle stems without breaking these in the process. Another method is to push a forked stick

So-called blanket weed, made up of slender threads of filamentous algae, grows on the surface of still water and can soon become unsightly. The algae thrive on sunlight and dissolved mineral salts that are often particularly plentiful in a new pool. If the growth becomes too vigorous before a natural balance is established, use a garden rake or rough stick to gather it up.

into a clump of blanket weed and, if this is rotated, the weed will be wound round the stick and can be pulled from the water.

Chemical methods of eradication are sometimes advised for bad infestation, but these can bring their own problems. If all else fails, empty the pool and, after scrubbing it out with a mild disinfectant, rinse and replant the pool including plenty of oxygenators. They are really the key to clear water and freedom from algae. You cannot have too many of them, especially during the early days when everything in the pool is settling down. Apart from absorbing dissolved mineral salts in the water, they cut down light, both of which deprive the algae of growth essentials. Natural shade will, in due course, be cast by floaters and the leaves of water-lilies, while goldfish help by consuming a small amount of algae in their diet.

Occasionally, in a large lake or pond underwater plants grow so thickly that it is impossible to see the base. However, the water will be crystal clear and the fish breed prolifically, finding food and protection in the masses of vegetation. Provided the plants remain submerged and are not annoying, they should be left alone. However one plant, a pondweed called *Potamogeton natans* will go on to produce floating leaves and brownish flowers of no great significance, both of which look unsightly *en masse.* These may have to be cut and dredged out of the water periodically, so the moral is, don't plant *Potamogeton natans* in the first place.

General problems

Water-lilies will not only fail to flower the first season, some kinds may even die if submerged too deeply directly after planting. Accordingly, lower them gradually into the water. Neither will they grow well in running water or too close to a fountain. In swift streams, use nuphars instead of nymphaeas and either keep water plants well away from fountain jets, or only play these infrequently.

If you want to safeguard your goldfish, refrain from putting pugnacious kinds like catfish and sticklebacks in the same pool. Also keep tench away from small pools if you want the water to stay clear. Overfeeding fish is another cause of cloudy water.

If cats or herons are a problem, spray a proprietary deterrent close to the pool edges (but not in the water) or adopt some of the suggestions mentioned previously (see page 33).

Pests

In late summer, blackfly often attack the

aerial parts of water-lilies and other aquatics in such numbers that they completely cover the stems and leaves. This causes discoloration and decay of the affected parts. Dislodge them with a powerful jet of water from a hose so that the blackfly fall into the pool, where they can be taken by fish. Since some always crawl back, repeat as necessary. Alternatively, submerge the water-lily leaves for 24 hours.

Caddis flies and mosquitoes may visit the pool during their breeding season. Both are a nuisance. The caddis fly larvae tear pieces of plant leaves to make pupae cases while the adult mosquitoes annoy people. With fish in the pool there is no occasion for worry.

Two other possible pests are the small brown china marks moth and the water-lily beetle. Both of these lay their eggs on water-lily leaves, which later provide food for their larvae. Eventually, this reduces everything to a brown rotting mass. Again, fish will devour them after the pests have been dislodged with a strong jet of water.

When autumn comes, a time-consuming task is the collection of leaves falling from trees and shrubs. They can be kept out of the water by means of a wire-mesh 'trap' laid across the pool surface. The leaves can then be gathered up regularly, without the worry of too much debris polluting the pool.

CHAPTER 5
FISH & WILDLIFE

The unique environment of a water garden will quickly attract a host of visitors both welcome and unwanted. As well as the natural wildlife, however, you will probably want to introduce a selection of fish to your pool.

Although it is not essential to have fish in a pool, there are various reasons for including them. For one thing they are delightful to watch as they dart from side to side, sometimes in schools on a 'follow my leader' basis, as is usual with golden orfe, or hovering near the surface in the case of goldfish. Fish bring life to the water garden, extending your reasons for wishing to visit it frequently and, if you feed them regularly in one place, they soon become tame enough to take food from your fingers.

They also help to provide a balanced environment, both for themselves and the pool plants. Their bodily waste fertilizes and feeds the latter, but in return fish need underwater vegetation on which to deposit their eggs and to hide the young fry which would otherwise be eaten after hatching. Most fish are cannibals.

When breathing, fish take in oxygen and exhale carbon dioxide, whereas plants use carbon dioxide in the process of manufacturing plant food but return oxygen to the water as a by-product of this process. Consequently both plants and fish utilize the waste products of the other and so form a mutually beneficial partnership.

Finally, fish protect plants from many of their enemies. They have voracious appetites and make short work of the larvae of mosquitoes and caddis flies, also snails' eggs and sundry small insects. Given the opportunity, they will even eat their own young.

The requirements of fish are few. They need a cool, shady area to retreat to in hot weather, such as that provided by the floating leaves of water-lilies, or a shelf under which they can hide. They also need sufficient water not to be overcrowded, otherwise they will be continually fighting for air.

Fish gasping at the surface are an indication of distress so it is important not to overstock the pool. Your dealer will be able to give an indication of the number you can accommodate, based on the size of your pool and its water capacity. As a rough guide, you can calculate that 2.5cm (1in) of fish needs 4.5 L (1 gal) of water. This means that a 7.5cm (3in) long fish will need 13.5 L (3 gal); a 23cm (9in) specimen 41 L (9 gal) and so on, but do make allowances for growth.

When purchased from a dealer the fish will probably be in a plastic bag. This will contain very little water, but just before it was sealed, oxygen will have been pumped inside – enough to prevent distress during travel. When you reach home, float the bag in the pool for half an hour, so that the water temperature inside this will become roughly the same as that in the pool. Now open the bag and turn it on its side so that the fish can swim out. This is better than netting, because it is less likely to frighten them or damage their scales.

Types of fish
The best kinds of fish to keep are those which have bright colours and also tend to live near the surface. They will coincidentally be the easiest to tame, as they should be constantly visible.

Goldfish
The undoubted pool favourites are goldfish, which are members of the carp family, and may be basically gold or variously patterned with red, gold, silver or black. They lay their eggs in early summer, most of the young fry appearing almost black when young and taking two or three years to assume their ultimate colouring.

Many varieties have been developed from the original species, mainly in the Orient, where they are extremely popular. One of these is the comet, which has typical goldfish colouring but a longer and slimmer body. It is a very quick mover and hardy enough to live in an outside pond.

Shubunkins are often known as calico fish because of their vivid hues and patternings. These include blues and mauves, whites and pinks or combinations of these. Those with a lot of blue colouring are the most sought after and also the most expensive. Shubunkins have few, if any, scales and are therefore more susceptible to bruising than ordinary goldfish, so treat them carefully. They will live outside in

A highly successful and popular fish for garden pools is the aptly named golden orfe. It is a lively and colourful species, typically feeding at the surface where it can be seen easily. As an added bonus, the golden orfe is a hardy fish that will survive cold weather without too much difficulty.

Golden orfe, golden carp, goldfish and golden rudd are all hardy and decorative fish for the garden pool. They bring life and movement to any water garden and will live together quite harmoniously.

sheltered places, but are best taken inside in late autumn if the pool is exposed or liable to severe freezing.

There are other goldfish variations such as elegant fantails; veiltails with long graceful tails which so slow down their speed that they appear to glide through the water; moors that are black in colour with protruding eyes; lionheads that have warty, cauliflower-like growths on their heads; and celestials, with upward poised eyes. None of these is really hardy enough for an outside pool and they are also extremely expensive. Accordingly, it is better to keep them in an indoor pool or aquarium.

Golden orfe
Golden orfe are exceptionally hardy and also very quick movers. Their slender, streamlined bodies cut through water with consummate ease. They are predominantly surface feeders and also swim in shoals, so they are visible for most of the day. Orfe are less vulnerable to disease than most pool fish, but they do need a fair sized pool, especially for breeding. If they have to be kept in a small pool, a fountain or running water should be installed during hot weather, otherwise they may die through lack of oxygen. Golden orfe are usually of a rich golden colour, sometimes with brownish flecks, but there is also a silver variety that is pale bluish-green above and silver beneath. Since orfe grow rather quickly, it is best to start with quite small specimens and watch them develop. In a large pool they will grow to 60cm (24in) in ten years.

Carp
Koi carp, also known as Nishiki Koi carp, make a handsome addition to any pool, over 6sq m (60sq ft) in size. They have been

cross-bred from different types of carp, resulting in fish of fantastic colourings. Some may be mostly yellow or pale gold, while others show a rainbow mixture of blues, reds, silvers, whites, golds and black. Those with the most vivid colours command very high prices. Koi carp are quite hardy and given plenty of space reach a large size – up to 1m (3ft) in length.

Common brown carp can be kept in pools but are less attractive than goldfish; they also tend to breed with goldfish and, in time, spoil the stock. The hi-goi carp is a form of common carp and either clear yellow or red, without spots or patches of other shades. Other carp include crucian carp, leather carp which are practically devoid of scales, and mirror carp which have patches of mirror-like scales on their bodies. Although good fish for lakes and similar large expanses of water, these carp are not suitable for small ornamental pools.

Tench
The common green tench and its golden form both have slippery bodies and both make good scavengers, but since they spend most of their lives on the floor of the pool they are rarely seen and constantly stir up sediment.

Rudd
Golden rudd are quick swimmers and often feed near the surface where their brilliant gold bodies and deep red fins made a surprising contrast. They need a fairly large pool or do not thrive.

Minnows
Minnows are delightful small fish, rarely more than 9cm (3½in) in length, and usually silver grey in colour with dark green backs and darker vertical bars. At breeding times, however, the male sports a red breast and has emerald-green sides. Minnows will eat mosquito or gnat larvae, also any natural fish food in the pond. They are essentially a river fish and prefer moving water, such as a stream, but will make do with a waterfall and circulating water or even a large pool with 60cm (24in) of water. In the nineteenth century, minnows were cultivated in this country for the table and were a great delicacy at banquets.

Fish to avoid
Do not be tempted to put into a garden pool fish caught in the wild, particularly pools already containing goldfish or other domestic fish. Not only do you risk introducing spores of disease or fish parasites with them, but the introduced fish may also be pugnacious carnivores.

Fish to avoid include perch, pike, stickle-

backs and catfish, all of which will bully other fish and, in many cases, devour them. Roach, which show a tendency to contract fungus disease, should also be avoided, as well as bream and green tench. The latter two spend their lives on the floor of the pond and constantly stir up mud and organic matter which leaves water cloudy.

Dace and trout need running water, well aerated, and again are not suitable for small pools.

Feeding
Most pool fish are carnivorous, eating both vegetable and protein foods. Although they can go for a long time without artificial food, sustaining themselves on whatever occurs naturally in the pool, they will not grow much nor will they breed successfully in a restricted space unless given additional food. All fish appreciate variety in their diet,

Though pool fish that occur in the wild can be attractive, they should not be added to a pool that contains 'domestic' species such as goldfish.
1 *The common tench stirs up sediment at the bottom of pools, making the water cloudy. The fish itself is only rarely seen.*
2 *Roach are best avoided because of their vulnerability to disease.*
3 *One of the most vicious carnivores, the pike will not only bully other fish but will also feed on them.*
4 *Another bully that should never be added to a garden pool is the perch.*

By feeding fish in the same place every day, they will quickly learn to gather there, giving you the chance to admire them properly. Some will even become tame enough to feed from the hand.

but only consume small quantities at a time so, with surface feeders like goldfish particularly, it is not only wasteful to give them too much, but unwise, since the remainder will sink to the bottom and decay. The golden rule is always to feed them in one place, providing just enough food for them to clear in five minutes. This, of course, does not apply when you provide live food, such as water fleas (daphnia) which can continue swimming about until ultimately eaten.

From late spring until early autumn, pool fish can be fed daily, but as winter approaches, the diet should be high in protein so that they can build up reserves of nourishment to tide them over from late autumn to late winter. The latter will be a period of fasting when no food at all should be provided, or the fish may contract digestive troubles. Meantime, if a few sunny days in winter tempt the fish to swim around, there will be enough natural food available for their needs.

Pet stores sell a wide range of dried fish foods, such as dried daphnia, dried brine shrimps and various pelleted proprietary foods scientifically formulated to provide a balanced diet. It is also possible to obtain frozen fish foods from dealers, such as tubifex worms, daphnia and shrimps. These can be kept in a deep freeze and small portions broken off as required. They should be thawed in cold water first and then emptied into the pool.

Fish troubles

Like all living creatures, fish can contract disease, although these rarely prove troublesome if the pool is well balanced. Prevention is always better than cure, so proper feeding, enough unpolluted water for the quantity of fish stocked and good planting are the best guarantees against infection. Avoid overstocking with fish; overfeeding; allowing a build up of organic matter from manures in the planting compost, fallen leaves and similar debris; introducing wild or unhealthy specimens or the careless use of weedkillers and sprays in the garden so that they drift or seep into the water.

Danger signs to observe are fish constantly gasping or gulping air near the surface; fish rolling on their sides in the water; fish rubbing themselves against the sides of the pool in an endeavour to get rid of parasites, or the appearance of a white, cotton-wool like mucus on their skins.

When troubles do occur, act quickly. If you see a dead fish remove it at once, otherwise it may be attacked by saprophytic fungi during the process of decomposition and pollute the water. The same thing applies to dead snails or other aquatic creatures, for it only takes a few hours for the corpses to become woolly all over with a coating of saprophytic fungi. When this happens it will prove impossible to discover the real killer.

Start by eliminating possible causes. Have sprays, lawn weedkillers, laburnum seeds or flowers (both poisonous) or even walnut leaves drifted into the water? These are all harmful and, if you feel any of these may be responsible, it may be necessary to change the water.

Do the fish have white or grey, cotton-wool like tufts adhering to their fins or bodies or, if the water is green, are there green growths looking like algae? If the answer is 'yes' it is probably fungus disease caused originally by some form of injury.

Cats, fish nets, bullying larger fish, overcrowding, exhaustion after travelling or abrupt changes in temperature could all be responsible. Contrary to popular belief, fungus disease is not infectious. It only attacks weak individuals, but if a number are infected, the cause must be sought and the pool treated, first by a slow water change and then by dosing it with proprietary algicide, used according to the the manufacturer's instructions. After 10 days, dose the pool again with a preventative proprietary substance. Both of these are obtainable from fish dealers. Any badly infected fish should be removed from the pool; concentrate on protecting the rest.

Various bacteria in the water may be responsible for other visible symptoms – tail rot, fin rot, red spots and patches and ulcers. If you see any of these, the pool water is probably unhygienic and infectious, so change the water and dose it with a preventative proprietary substance.

If fish keep gulping at the surface they are probably short of oxygen. Get rid of the surplus carbon dioxide in the water, which is gradually poisoning them, by playing a fountain or pumping water through a waterfall for up to 24 hours. If you do not have either of these, splash water from a hose very vigorously on the surface or, better still, use an inexpensive aquarium pump for a few days in order to get some oxygen into the pool. Incidentally, aquarium pumps are not designed to go outdoors, so house them somewhere under cover. A plastic air line linking pool and pump will cause bubbling and agitation in the pool when the pump is turned on, bringing air into the water.

Flukes, fish lice and a creature called the anchor worm sometimes attack fish on their bodies and gills, making breathing difficult and leaving the victims pale and listless. However, if treated early, these parasites can be destroyed. Dose the pool with proprietary medicinal compound several times, at intervals of a few days. Orfe react adversely to medicinal compounds, so these should not be used when orfe are present.

Fish attacked by flukes can often be seen rubbing themselves against the sides of the pool in an endeavour to dislodge the pests. Later, as the infestation builds up, the fins may fold under, bloody patches will appear on the skin and the fish swim about slowly. Some of these parasites are too small to be seen with the naked eye, although leeches will be visible and can usually be removed with tweezers.

Other pool creatures

There was a time when water snails were looked upon as essential to the well being of a pool. This was because of their scavenging habits and the fact that they would consume small quantities of algae. However, nowadays, they are looked upon less favourably.

Many kinds will eat plants as well as algae, including the submerged oxygenators. They also breed at an alarming rate, laying their eggs in unpleasant-looking, jelly-like masses on the undersides of water lily leaves. The leaves are later nibbled by the emerging young.

Snails also use up oxygen in the water and produce carbon dioxide. They play host to various parasites and will eat fish eggs as well as fish food.

Admittedly their own eggs and very young snails are also eaten by fish, but this does not compensate for the harm they do. Consequently it is unwise to introduce them to a new pool, but if they are present and in quantities sufficient to cause problems, many can be trapped by placing a cabbage stump in the water. Leave this overnight and the next morning take it out and shake off the adhering snails. Repeat as necessary.

Frogs, toads and newts are amphibians which spend most of their lives on land but seek water at breeding time. There is no point in introducing them to the garden pool. If they are in the vicinity they will probably visit it in spring. Very rarely a male frog or toad has been known to grip a slow-moving fish so tightly that it kills the fish, but this only occurs when there are surplus males in the pool and most fish keep well out of their way.

The tadpoles are good scavengers and nibble at algae until such time as they produce legs, when they become more interested in protein foods and insects. In the meantime, frog tadpoles (toad tadpoles are rejected) make live food for fishes.

Newts can feed under water and generally return annually to the same breeding ponds, a practice repeated by their offspring with quite amazing determination. They can eat very young goldfish but are unlikely to harm adult specimens.

Various flying insects may be attracted to the pool in summer. Some, such as bees and wasps, are harmless and only come to drink. Others, such as dragonflies and water beetles, lay their eggs nearby and their larvae or nymphs can be very destructive both to plants and fish. Water boatmen, whirligig and diving beetles as well as water scorpions can sometimes be seen darting about the water, and even those which feed predominantly on other insects will sometimes attack small fish. Although they cannot be avoided and will come to a pool uninvited, if any are seen, they can be netted and destroyed.

Top *Water snails are generally thought of as being welcome inhabitants of a pool but, in fact, they can do more harm than good. Here, the great Ramshorn snail (Planorbus cornelus) feeds underwater on the leaves of frogbit (Hydrocharis morsus-ranae).*

Above left *The common frog is becoming an increasingly familiar sight in garden pools.*

Above *Though dragonfly larvae are destructive, the adults are both delicate and beautiful. Here, a Dragonfly rests with wings outstretched in the sun.*

CHAPTER 6

WATER GARDEN CALENDAR

Although water gardens are relatively trouble-free, they do need regular maintenance. By following a simple time-table, you can be certain that all the necessary tasks are completed in good time.

There are some garden features that demand attention all through the year, but the water garden is not one of them. It certainly has periods of great activity, but also times when the pace slackens and it is possible to sit by the pool to enjoy the movement of water, the antics of the fish, and admire the plants.

The following calendar not only gives some reminders of the various tasks to be undertaken, but also suggests aquatics and bog plants for different seasons.

Spring

This is the most active season and an important time for planting up new pools and cleaning out old ones.

Construct new prefabricated pools in an open, sunny place, after taking out excavations slightly deeper than seems necessary. Tamp the base to make it firm, cover with 2.5cm (1in) of sand or sifted ashes and insert the pool. Test for levels and fill with water.

Prepare sites for pool liners in the same way, line excavations with the material and fill with water. Cut off surplus lining material except for 15cm (6in) all round the edges. Tuck this out of sight and conceal with paving or plants.

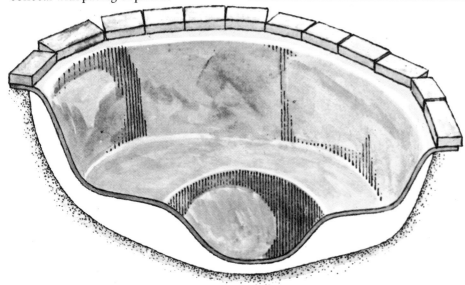

Above *When using a pool liner, make the profile an irregular shape.*
Left *Fibreglass moulds are easy to install.*
Below *Water-lilies are planted in baskets.*

Above *To divide water-lilies, cut away growing tips and plant separately.*

Plant water-lilies and other deep water aquatics in mid-spring. Top-dress their containers with shingle and sink these into the water.

Plant underwater oxygenators and marginal aquatics.

Install fish after two weeks.

If necessary, lift water-lilies in mid or late spring. It is worth doing this if they have been planted for more than four years. Wash the roots, cut away old parts of the tuber and re-plant young pieces, each with a strong shoot and about 15cm (6in) of attached tuber. Use fresh loam and bone-meal for planting compost.

Clean out old or dirty pools. Retain some of the best plants and discard the rest, along with the old soil. Scrub the pond, using either enough permanganate of potash to turn the water pink, or a mild disinfectant. Rinse, leave to dry out, then re-plant.

From early spring begin feeding fish as they become active.

Tidy and remove dead pieces of water plants killed during the winter.

Clean existing bog gardens, removing large weeds by hand. Hoe around plants and install new ones.

New bog gardens may be planted in mid-spring. Set the smaller plants in groups of three or five (more if you have the space), for maximum effect.

Plant *Calla palustris* and *Menyanthes trifoliata* roots horizontally in mud near the pool edges.

Plant bog plants from early to mid-spring.

Divide existing clumps of perennials.

Plants to enjoy in spring
Acorus (sweet flag), alnus, caltha (kingcup), *Hottonia palustris,*

lysichitum, menyanthes, metasequoia, orontium (golden club), peltiphyllum (umbrella plant), primula, ranunculus, salix, saururus (lizard's tail), scirpus (bullrushes), trollius (globe flowers).

Summer
Though not the time for any major tasks, routine checks will ensure that fish and plants stay healthy.

Remove scum from a new pool by drawing newspaper across its surface, or else flood it over with water from a hose.

To help fish in very hot or stormy weather, play a fountain or waterfall if you have them, using a pump to re-cycle the water.

Keep a sharp look-out for aphids on water-lily leaves or the foliage of marginal aquatics. Hose them into the water for the fish to take. For bad infestations, sink water-lily leaves beneath the water overnight by weighting them down with something heavy like a hoop.

If snails are chewing foliage, trap them with a cabbage stump or old lettuce plant.

Put in more oxygenating plants if water is discoloured.

Control algae if necessary (see page 39).

From time to time replace water lost by evaporation.

Left Lysichitum americanum *is a striking plant for the waterside.*
Below *The common pond snail.*

Cut off and remove old water-lily leaves and flowers.

Finish planting aquatics and bog plants before the end of early summer.

Keep the bog garden weeded, also watered if necessary.

Regularly deadhead flowers and remove dead leaves in the bog garden.

Keep inveterate self-seeders from becoming invasive by removing flowers soon after they fade.

Save seeds of primulas and sow immediately in boxes of good compost. Keep in a cold frame.

In early summer, put out water hyacinths, floating these on the surface of the pool.

Watch for cats, herons and other birds visiting the pool to catch fish.

Feed the fish regularly and in the same place.

Save seed of any special bog plants.

Thin oxygenating plants if necessary.

Plants to enjoy in summer
Acorus (sweet flag), alisma (water plantain), aponogeton (water hawthorn), astilbe, butomus (flowering rush), cimicifuga, eichhornia (water hyacinth), filipendula (meadowsweet),

Below Iris kaempferi *revels in moist soil.*
Right *and* **top** *In autumn, feed fish on high protein food such as worms. Check that the pool heater is working and install it once autumn debris is cleared (bottom right). Use the old leaves of* Gunnera manicata *to protect the plant crowns (bottom).*

Gentiana lutea, glyceria (manna grass), gunnera, hydrangea, *Hypericum elodes*, iris, juncus (corkscrew rush), lobelia, mimulus (monkey musk), myosotis (water forget-me-not), orontium (golden club), primula, ranunculus, rodgersia, sagittaria, stratiotes (water cactus), zantedeschia (arum lily).

Autumn

As the year advances, dead leaves should be gathered regularly and preparations made for the cold months ahead.

In autumn, lift a few of the smaller water hyacinths, pot these in soil fairly close together in a bowl, add a little water and store in a light, frost-free place.

Dredge fallen leaves from the pool, or better still, cover the water surface with mesh netting to trap them.

In mid-autumn feed the fish heavily with a protein food such as water fleas, worms, or proprietary foods. Cease feeding altogether at the end of late autumn.

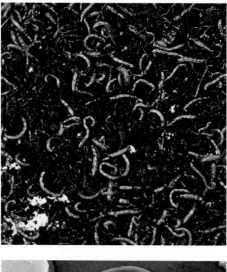

Cut down dead vegetation at the waterside.

In late autumn overhaul the pumps used for fountains and waterfalls. Remove submersible types from the water, clean and store dry.

Protect gunneras by cutting off leaves as soon as these are touched by frost and inverting them over plant crowns. Add a little hay or straw if the position is exposed.

In early autumn, gather materials for dried arrangements from bog and water plants: iris seedheads, grasses, reedmace, hydrangea flowers, and the like.

Lift a few plants of *Lobelia fulgens* and store in a cold frame all winter. They may go through satisfactorily outdoors, but this precaution safeguards the stock. Repeat with any plants you are doubtful about, or protect them with dry leaves over the crowns.

Above *Over-winter young and dwarf water-lilies by keeping in a frost-free place.*
Left Aponogeton distachys, *the water hawthorn, has white flowers.*

You can make a pool now, but avoid frosty weather. Leave the completed pool full of water all winter.

In mid-autumn plant fresh plants in the bog garden.

Lift miniature water-lilies in shallow rock pools, plant in loam in a bowl, and over-winter inside away from frost.

Plant bluebell and narcissus bulbs in the bog garden for extra colour.

Plants to enjoy in autumn or early winter

Aponogeton (water hawthorn), calla berries, cimicifuga (bugbane), decodon (for autumnal tints), eriophorum (cotton grass), *Gentiana asclepiadea*, hydrangea, kirengeshoma, lythrum, pernettya, schizostylis, sorbaria, typha (reed mace).

Winter

Some repair work can be done on warm days and steps taken to protect plants and fish against more severe weather.

Keep the pool full of water.

Float a ball or block of wood in the pool. If ice forms 2.5cm (1in) or more thick, pour boiling water over the ball and

Right *Winter tip: A rubber ball on the water of the pool.*

remove. Bale out 2.5cm (1in) of water and cover the hole with a thick sack. Top up with water after every thaw. Repeat as necessary.

Sow seeds of bog plants and aquatics early in the year, but keep under glass.

Dredge out leaves or any debris likely to rot in the pool.

Check doubtfully hardy bog plants and protect with cloches, or dry leaves and polythene.

Protect small rock plants with boards and straw matting.

Repair pools in frost-free weather.

Below *Repair concrete pools in early winter when there is no danger of frost.*

1

2

CHAPTER 7
WATER PLANT GUIDE

Water plants can be both beautiful and practical: they bring colour and style to the most luxurious gardens and play an important part in ensuring that the pool itself is a healthy environment.

Having considered the various types of pool, how to make them, the fish that swim in them, and the various other creatures that breed in or are attracted to water, it is time to consider the plants.

For many gardeners, plants are the *raison d'être* of the water garden; they give it both distinction and charm. The range of plants that can be grown in and around the pool is considerable and often not fully exploited.

Mention a pool and most people immediately think of water-lilies, and it cannot be denied that these are the choicest aquatics to grow, but a well-planted pool will contain different types of plants. Besides the deep-water plants, having their roots completely submerged but the leaves and flowers floating on the surface, there should be submerged aquatics, floating plants, and the 'marginals' to grow at the edge of the pool.

Submerged aquatics
Some of these plants spend the whole of their lives submerged, and a few will even flower beneath the surface. Others may hover at or just below the surface, but at flowering time produce aerial stems carrying one or several blooms above the water. These differences are connected with their methods of pollination, for while the male spores of some reach the female flowers by water, others depend on wind or insects to achieve pollination.

Most submerged aquatics have soft foliage, usually cut or shredded into fine segments, through which water can flow without injury to the leaf blades. The plants are thus well adapted to water in all its moods, including running water and flooding. Because all submerged aquatics need carbon-dioxide for photosynthesis (the process by which plants convert light into energy), they utilize the gases breathed out by fish during respiration and therefore help to keep the water in balance. Conversely, fish must have oxygen and, since this is discharged into the pool by the plants as a by-product of photosynthesis, this also helps fish and various other types of animal life.

Because all submerged plants produce oxygen in this manner they are known as 'oxygenating plants' and will be found under that heading on page 59.

Floaters
Some aquatics spend their lives free and unanchored. During the growing season they float on the water and are carried hither and thither by its movement, a circumstance which accounts for their spread, particularly in the tropics where water hyacinths, water lettuces and salvinias (all susceptible to frost) are often a menace. Even in northern countries like Britain, duckweed can present problems.

Some floaters form 'turons' (winter buds) in autumn, a device which protects them from cold and ice. The turons then sink to the floor of the pool and overwinter in mud. When the water warms up in spring they grow again and rise to the surface.

The importance of floaters lies in the shade they cast, which is important to fish in summer, and helps to reduce algae, which need sunlight to thrive. Their tangled and dangling roots provide hiding places for myriads of small water insects and thus act as fish larders.

Marginal aquatics
As their name implies, marginal plants only need shallow water. The roots are submerged most of the time, while the leaves and flowers grow up and out of the water. Many marginal plants are highly ornamental, with attractive flowers or foliage. They break the flat outlines of a pool, relieving it of formality and, if carefully selected, provide long-term interest and a range of plant heights. Nearly all thrive in heavy loam and can be planted in spring or early summer.

Bog plants
This section includes a miscellany of plants that will survive in wet, boggy soil for some or part of the time, and plants that like to feel the influence of water without actually sitting in it. In other words they need damp but not waterlogged conditions. Many of

Well known for their large, rounded leaves and many-petalled, cup-shaped flowers, the water-lilies (Nymphaea varieties) are undoubted favourites in any garden pool.

these plants are frequently seen in borders, like *Iris sibirica*, trollius, and astilbes. Given sufficient moisture in summer they often do well in such situations, but when droughts occur the story is different. In the vicinity of a pool, which can be flooded over when necessary, or when grown in a bog garden, they never suffer privation and always make fine specimens.

Some bog plants have brilliant flowers, others have quaint practices such as catching insects in the case of sarracenias. There are even a few bulbs and trees that will live under conditions of poor drainage such as would kill most garden plants.

Deep water plants

Although it is always worth trying to find room for a range of deep water plants (see page 58), water-lilies are such attractive members of this group they will probably be the first plants pool owners will consider.

Water-lilies

The genus *Nymphaea* is widespread, with representation in most countries, particularly in the tropics although there is even one in Arctic Finland. As well as white and cream water-lilies there are pink, red, yellow and blue, most of them day bloomers but a few are night flowering. There is also a wide variation in flower sizes – from a tea plate down to miniatures small enough to slip through a wedding ring.

Water-lilies are also interesting historically, having been venerated as emblems of regeneration and purity since the times of the Pharaohs.

This symbolism was apparently linked with their annual emergence from the mud and slime of dried up pools, once they became refilled by the flood waters of the Nile. The esteem in which they were held by the Ancient Egyptians also led to their use in funeral wreaths and chaplets (this was particularly common during the 19th and 21st dynasties). Petals of *Nymphaea caerulea* were found with the mummies of both Rameses II and Amenhotep.

Many well-known symbols also have associations with water-lilies. According to Professor Goodyear (Grammar of the Lotus) the ramshorn motif of the Ionic capital owes its origin to their twisted sepals, and from that was derived the Greek fret, which doubled again became the swastika. This very early symbol, which is portrayed on many Egyptian murals and ornaments, represents light or darkness, good or evil, death or life – according to the directions assumed by the arms. Apart from such symbolical associations the starchy rhizomes of various water-lilies have been consumed as food by Africans, North American Indians, and even Europeans in times of want. The Scots obtained a brown dye from the roots of *N. alba*, and the soft moist leaves are used in tropical countries for poultices.

The common white water-lily of Britain is *N. alba*, a vigorous plant that is able to take deeper water than most of the garden hybrids commonly sold for pools. In the 1800's a red sport of this species appeared in a lake in Sweden and became important as the first red form known to Europeans.

Credit for the wealth of colours now available is due to the tenacity and hybridizing genius of a Frenchman called Joseph Bory Latour Marliac. In 1858, reading an article in *La Revue du Jardin des Plants de Paris* about some new, brightly coloured tropical nymphaeas then growing at the Museum of Natural History, Marliac thought how marvellous it would be if the waterways of France could be planted with variously coloured, hardy water-lilies. Accordingly he started a hobby, which was to become the work of a lifetime, and set out to produce them.

The red form of *N. alba* was one of his early acquisitions, and was followed by a yellow, *N. mexicana* from Mexico, pinks from North America and various blue and red tropicals. Through the years Marliac worked on his water-lilies, crossing and recrossing the species and varieties until by the end of the century he was reaping rich rewards. Plant followed plant in quick succession until eventually the parentage of many became an enigma. Nor did he ever disclose his hybridizing methods and with his death in 1911 any prospect of discovering them vanished.

Nearly all the hardy water-lilies grown today owe their origin to Marliac's genius. Although he never achieved his ambition of producing a blue, hardy variety, he has left us a legacy of varieties which no-one will ever surpass.

Early water-lilies need heavy loam and should be planted in aquatic baskets as described on page 36.

When it comes to choosing varieties it is important to select kinds that are suitable both for the depth and available growing space. To make the choice easier, each variety described has the letter A, B or C (explained below) following the description to indicate its size and vigour:

A. *Vigorous varieties* for depths of 60-100cm (24-36in) and surface areas around 0.50-0.75sq m (5-8sq ft). For large ponds and lakes.

B. *Medium growers* for depths of 45-60cm (18-24in) and surfaces areas around 0.25–0.5 sq m (3–6 sq ft). Generally

*Opposite There is a wide range of water-lilies (*Nymphaea *spp.) to choose from, especially if you visit a specialist grower.*
1 N. lactea, *an attractive garden variety has white flowers with warm, golden centres.*
2 *'Gonnêre' is a handsome white, with double flowers. It is suitable for water up to 38cm (15in) deep.*
3 *'Sunrise', is one of the finest yellow water-lilies and is best in water up to 60cm (24in) deep.*
4 *The more tender varieties boast some of the most beautiful flowers (here, 'Director G. T. Moore') but they need special care through the winter months.*
5 *The 'Laydekeri' hybrids include many varieties listed either in their main colour groups or as named forms such as 'Laydekeri Fulgens', shown here.*
6 N. Amabilis *a variably coloured water-lily, has pink-flushed outer petals.*
7 *The delightful, dwarf yellow flowers of* N. pygmaea *'Helvola' here contrast well with those of another charming small water lily.*

suitable for small and medium pools.

C. *Small and miniature* varieties for 23-38cm (9-15in) depths. Suitable for tubs, rock pools and small prefabricated pools, but may need some protection in winter for the shallower depths.

Selecting water-lilies

There are many water-lily varieties, some rare, some common, some prolific bloomers, some shy flowering. The following varieties, graded according to colour, are normally available from specialist growers. The letters at the end of the descriptions refer to the planting depths mentioned in the previous code. When two numbers are quoted it indicates that the variety is adaptable to both sets of conditions. The letter N before the name denotes the genus *Nymphaea*, and is followed by the species name.

White

N. alba. The common white water-lily, only suitable for very large areas. A.

'Albatross'. White with gold stamens, young leaves purple, turning green with age. B.

N. candida. Small flowers, very hardy, white with red stigmas. C.

'Caroliniana Nivea'. Fragrant, larger than preceding. C.

'Gladstoniana'. Possibly the best white, very large flowers, 15-20cm (6-8in) across with rich, golden stamens. A.

'Gonnêre'. Squat, double-white with prominent green sepals. A/B.

N. 'Marliacea Albida'. Popular white, very free flowering; slightly fragrant. B.

N. odorata. The fragrant white water-lily of North America. Medium-sized flowers. B.

N. pygmaea alba. Small white flowers under 5cm (2in) across. Can be raised from seed. Needs shallow water (around 15cm/6in). C.

N. tuberosa 'Richardsonii'. Globular white flowers with green sepals; vigorous. B/C.

Pink

'Amabilis'. Star-like, soft pink flowers, deepening to salmon-rose. B.

'Brakleyi Rosea'. Splendid deep rose-pink, free flowering and fragrant. B.

'Colossea'. Soft pinkish-white, very large flowers. Vigorous. A.

'Fire Crest'. Wide, deep-pink, fragrant flowers with prominent-red-tipped stamens. B/C.

N. 'Laydekeri Lilacea'. Very free flowering, soft rosy-lilac deepening with age to rose. B/C.

N. 'Marliacea Carnea'. Pale flesh-pink,

very shapely; reliable and free flowering. A/B.

N. 'Marliacea Rosea'. Similar to preceding but with richer pink colouring which sometimes does not develop fully until the second season. Fragrant. A/B.

'Masaniello'. A popular variety with sweetly scented, large, cup-shaped, deep rose flowers. B/C.

'Mme Wilfron Gonnêre'. Large, double, rose-pink. Not so free flowering as some varieties. B.

'Mrs Richmond'. Large, globular, rich pink blooms, deepening in colour towards centre. B.

N. odorata 'Turicensis'. Soft rose, free flowering, sweetly scented. C.

N. odorata 'W. B. Shaw'. Flowers cup-shaped, delicate pink, deeper inside. B/C.

'Rose Arey'. An outstanding, rich rose-pink with large star-like flowers that have slightly incurved petals; fragrant and free flowering. B.

N. tuberosa 'Rosea'. Vigorous and fragrant. Soft pink. A.

Red

'Attraction'. Large, glowing, garnet-red flowers 17-20cm (7-8in) across, tipped with white. A/B.

'Charles de Meurville'. A vigorous variety with wine-red flowers produced over a long season. A/B.

'Conqueror'. Flowers blood-red with white inside the sepals; these often stay open at night. B.

'Escarboucle'. Excellent ruby-red with huge blooms as large as tea plates; reliable and consistent. B.

'Froebeli'. Deep wine-red flowers, free flowering. C.

'James Brydon'. One of the best, and extremely free flowering. Blooms rich carmine-red, sitting squat in the water. Young leaves purple. B.

N. 'Laydekeri Purpurata'. Extremely free flowering and a great favourite for tubs and small ponds. Medium-sized, wine-red flowers. B/C.

'Newton'. Star-shaped blooms held slightly above the water, rosy vermilion with orange stamens. B.

'René Gerard'. Rich rose, star-shaped flowers up to 23cm (9in) across. These are flecked and striped with red crimson. Free flowering. B.

N. pygmaea 'Rubra'. Rose-pink flowers 6cm (2½in) across, deepening to red with age; foliage green. C.

'William Falconer'. Very dark red with yellow stamens. B.

Yellow

'Colonel A. J. Welch'. Very vigorous, but a

The delicate pink, cup-shaped blooms of N. odorata 'W. B. Shaw' are set off by showy, golden stamens.

shy bloomer. Flowers canary-yellow held just above the water. A.

N. 'Marliacea Chromatella'. Soft yellow flowers of fine shape; bright yellow stamens. One of the best yellows. Foliage chocolate-blotched. B.

'Moorei'. Very similar to preceding but foliage spotted rather than blotched. B.

N. odorata 'Sulphurea'. Small, deep yellow blooms, often standing just clear of the water; blotched leaves. C.

N. pygmaea 'Helvola'. A little charmer, soft, sulphur-yellow, 5cm (2in) across; maroon-blotched leaves. Very free flowering if left undisturbed. Grow in water 10-15cm (4-6in) deep.

'Sunrise'. Deep sunshine-yellow, the richest in colour, large and slightly fragrant. Foliage green flecked brown, red beneath. B.

Variable colours

'Graziella'. Reddish-yellow flowers, becoming paler with age; foliage variegated with purple. C.

'Indiana'. Flowers open apricot-red, gradually darkening to rich copper-red; foliage suffused with purple. B/C.

'Paul Hariot'. Flowers first apricot-yellow then orange-pink and finally almost red; maroon-spotted foliage. Very free flowering. B/C.

'Sioux'. Soft yellow suffused with red, deepening to reddish-copper.

'Solfaterre'. Flowers star-shaped, yellow flushed rose; foliage green mottled with maroon. B/C.

All these hardy water-lilies can be increased by dividing the tubers in early spring. The bulk of the old roots should be discarded, retaining only the young crowns with 7.5-10cm (3-4in) of new tuber.

Very small pieces can be grown on to flower the following season. Pot these in plain loam and stand them in a deep bowl of water with the crowns barely covered. Keep in a light place under cover. Re-pot if necessary and increase the water depth but do not plant outside until the following spring.

Tropical water-lilies are only rarely available in Britain and they are not easy to grow. Our summers are not sufficiently warm for their comfort and, even when

The carmine-red flowers of 'James Brydon' float on water almost completely covered by its maroon-splashed leaves.

started in tanks of shallow water under glass, when put outside and temperatures drop lower than 21°C (70°F), the plants stop growing.

It is also necessary to lift them in autumn when they die down, and store the tubers under cover all winter.

If you want tropical nymphaeas – and they are undeniably beautiful – with blue, purple, and yellow varieties as well as reds, pinks and whites, you will need an indoor pool, with extra heating in cold weather.

In many respects they are quite different from hardy water-lilies. The flowers stand on stiff stems well above the water surface, the rootstock is smaller and almost bulb-like, the new plant growing on top and replacing the old after a period of rest. Most tropical water-lilies produce viable seed – whereas nearly all the hardy varieties are sterile; many are richly scented; others bloom at night and some species and varieties are viviparous, developing baby plantlets on their leaves, like the well-known house plant *Tolmiea menziesii*.

Other deep water plants

Nuphars, sometimes known as pond lilies, are extremely hardy and vigorous aquatics, similar to nymphaeas but inferior. The European, including British, *N. lutea* is often called brandy bottle because of the vinous scent of its small bright yellow flowers. It produces two kinds of leaves, oval to heart-shaped, leathery floating leaves and – in deep or running water – crisped, translucent leaves.

Nuphars are useful for deep water, running streams or shady ponds – all places where nymphaeas are unlikely to succeed. But they are rampant, so plant with care.

Below Nuphar lutea *is also known as the yellow water-lily or, more popularly, the brandy bottle.*

Below right *Water milfoil* (Myriophyllum spicatum), *with its feathery floating leaves, is an excellent oxygenating plant.*

The only nuphars worth growing are the less invasive *N. advena* 'Variegata' which has cream and green, variegated leaves, and *N. japonica rubrotincta* with red-tipped stamens and orange-scarlet flowers.

The water hawthorn, or caltha *Aponogeton distachyus*, is a charmer from South Africa with floating, strap-like leaves and vanilla-scented white flowers with jet-black anthers. These are grouped in forked inflorescences that float on or just above the surface of the water.

The flowering season of the water hawthorn is long, from mid or late spring until autumn; I have even picked blooms on Christmas Day and occasionally in March. The chestnut-sized tubers should be planted in loam and will adapt to 45cm (18in) of water but flower better in 15-23cm (6-9in). This is a plant for every pond, large or small.

Oxygenating plants

The importance of oxygenating plants has already been stressed but, because their ability to produce oxygen is largely linked with their rate of growth, it is important to select efficient kinds.

There is a new and growing practice by dealers of offering plants which are not submerged aquatics, but bog or even house plants. Usually these are recommended for aquaria, where they may look pretty through the glass sides for a few weeks, but they will not oxygenate the water.

Aquaria of course can have oxygen supplied by pumps, and pools by fountains, but oxygenating plants have other functions. They provide somewhere for fish to lay their eggs and are a sanctuary for the young fry. They also play a useful role in keeping down algae and other weeds.

Really efficient oxygenators are the starworts *Callitriche* spp., which remain submerged for much of the time but come to the surface to produce their insignificant flowers. They are easily recognized at such times by their small, light green, floating leaves, which form starry masses. The autumn starwort is most effective at that season and the spring starwort in spring, so it is advisable to stock both.

Elodea canadensis or Canadian pondweed, with close whorls of small leaves on branching stems and the larger, curly-leaved *Lagarosiphon major* (often sold as *Elodea crispa*) are two splendid oxygenators. They are hardy and submerged at all seasons. Milfoils (*Myriophyllum spp.*) with needle-fine leaves arranged in whorls, are also effective, as are certain pondweeds like *Potamogeton crispus* and *P. densus*.

Several oxygenators come to the surface

to flower, like the water crowfoot *(Ranunculus aquatilis)* with small white, starry buttercup flowers; the water violet *(Hottonia palustris)*, which produces whorls of pale purple flowers on 7.5-10cm (3-4in) spikes; and the bladderwort *(Utricularia vulgaris)*, a native insectivorous plant that traps water fleas and in summer produces spikes of yellow, snapdragon-like flowers.

Floaters

This is not a large group and fewer still are hardy. The smaller kinds are often eaten by fishes, which with duckweed is an advantage. There are several kinds of duckweeds, none of which should ever be introduced into ornamental ponds.

The frogbit *(Hydrocharis morsus-ranae)* has rosettes of fleshy and rounded floating leaves, each about 2.5cm (1in) across, and with trailing roots and white, three-petalled flowers.

Fairy floating mosses (*Azolla* spp.) do

Hottonia palustris, *the water violet, can be relied upon to oxygenate the water and is both attractive and practical in a garden pool.*

Despite its delightful flowers, the water hyacinth (Eichhornia crassipes) *is notorious for rampant growth that can quickly choke large stretches of water. It is not a hardy plant, however, and cold weather will check this growth naturally.*

indeed look like pale green mosses in summer, but turn red in autumn before most are killed by frost. Generally a few survive between the stems of marginal plants, however, and maintain the stock.

The water soldier or water cactus (*Stratiotes aloides*) bobs about like a pineapple top just beneath the water, but thrusts its way upwards to flower. The blooms are white and three-petalled, male and female on separate plants.

The water hyacinth (*Eichhornia crassipes*) is fortunately, perhaps, not hardy in Britain, for under congenial conditions it spreads rapidly by means of runners. It forms large mats of smooth round leaves, with sausage-like swollen leaf stalks full of spongy tissue that keep the plant afloat. Spectacular spikes of showy blue flowers with gold and dark blue peacock markings on the upper petals appear in summer. Long black roots about 30cm (12in) long, hang down in the water and keep the plants balanced. If you aim to grow this plant do not put it outside until mid-June when all danger of frost has passed, and always overwinter a few small plants in a bowl inside to retain the stock.

Two other tender floaters are sometimes grown in small pools and overwintered in the same manner. They are the water lettuce (*Pistia stratiotes*), which does indeed resemble a velvety miniature lettuce, and the water velvets (*Salvinia* spp.), which are fern allies with distinctive ear-shaped, unwettable leaves covered with fine silky hairs.

Marginals

Marginal aquatics are mainly for decorative purposes, making an attractive setting for a pond in the same way that trees and shrubs embellish a garden. Accordingly they should be planted with a view to providing long-term interest and never allowed to become so rampant that they hide the water. You might find it useful to look at the seasonal advice in Chapter Six to ensure that you have marginals that will provide flowers or other features of interest spread over most of the season.

Marginal plants can be grown in pockets or troughs built into the sides of artificial pools, or in aquatic baskets (as for water-lilies) or similar containers. They can even be planted in soil at the sides of a natural pond. A depth of 5-10cm (2-4in), and a plain loam compost, is suitable for most. It is advisable to cover the soil with a dressing of washed shingle to stop fish rooting into it.

Strong and rampant growers will need lifting and dividing from time to time – approximately every third year. Nearly all the plants in this section can be increased by division in spring; exceptions are noted in the text.

Acorus calamus, the sweet flag, is so called because its iris-like leaves and rootstock are highly aromatic when bruised. This circumstance, in Tudor times, led to its leaves being used (instead of rushes) for strewing floors in wealthy homes. The powdered root is still employed for scenting hair and tooth powders, and as an insect repellent. Calamus oil, distilled from the plant, is used to flavour various kinds of beer as well as gin and bitters.

The sweet flag, in spite of its iris appearance, is an aroid and at flowering time, short conical inflorescences (looking like miniature cattle horns), are produced near the tips of the flower stems. The species grows 60-100cm (24-36in) tall but is best represented by the white and green variegated form 'Variegata'. *A. gramineum* is dwarfer at 20-30cm (8-12in) and very slender, forming compact grassy tufts, either in wet soil or very shallow water. It, too, is most worthwhile when planted in its variegated form.

Water plantains (*Alisma* spp.) have long stemmed, plantain-like leaves and whorls of tiny, three-petalled, rosy-lilac flowers on pyramidal 30-45cm (12-18in) stems. Unfortunately they are inveterate seeders, so the old flower heads should be removed regularly before the seed is shed. The best for water gardens are *A. gramineum* with oblong leaves, or the great water plantain *A. plantago-aquatica*, for large stretches of water. Neither species will flower well except in very shallow water.

The flowering rush, *Butomus umbellatus*, is a British native occasionally found near stream edges or in wet pastures. It grows 60-100cm (24-36in) tall with narrow, smooth green leaves, which are purplish when young, and umbels of pink three-petalled flowers. It makes quite a show when grouped in water 5-15cm (2-6in) deep. The baked roots are esteemed as a vegetable in Northern Asia.

Calla palustris is the bog arum. Although unrelated, except in a broad family sense, it looks like the arum lily (*Zantedeschia*), with small white flowers and shiny, dark green, heart-shaped leaves. If pollinated, which is carried out by water snails, the flowers go on to produce globular clusters of red berries. The bog arum is a scrambling plant with creeping rhizomes. It never grows more than about 23cm (9in) high, but wends its way skilfully between shallow water and wet soil; a circumstance which makes it a useful plant for masking the edges of artificial pools.

Marsh marigold and kingcup, or 'water blob' in northern Britain, are all names for

Above left Caltha palustris, *'Flore Pleno',* is the double form of the marsh marigold **(above)**: *both plants thrive in moist conditions and will flourish at the water's edge.*

Caltha palustris. It is one of our handsomest spring flowers, bearing masses of 2.5cm (1in) bright golden, buttercup-like flowers on branching stems, and entire, rounded, tooth-edged leaves. During the last century the young stems and leaves were apparently eaten by country people as spring greens and the flowers buds were pickled as a substitute for capers. But the sap has the poisonous constituents of buttercups and this is not recommended. Animals tend to avoid marsh marigolds, which is also a strong warning against the idea.

The double marigold 'Flore Pleno', or 'Monstrosa' as it is known in the United States, is particularly free flowering, usually masking the leaves and stems with dozens of golden, button-like flowers.

Most marsh marigolds bloom around mid-spring, but the taller *C. polypetala* blooms several weeks later. This is a particularly fine plant with wide spreading branches carrying the blooms. It reaches about 1m (3ft). There are also white species such as *C. leptosepala,* but these do far better in damp soil than water.

Cotula coronopifolia, a pretty little plant that associates charmingly with blue water forget-me-nots, is only recommended for wet soil or shallow water in a warm, sheltered pool. Since the round golden flowers resemble the middle disc of a daisy – with the white outer florets removed – it is commonly known as brass buttons. It grows about 15-23cm (6-9in) high and the smooth, toothed leaves smell of lemons when crushed. The plant is an annual but in a warm summer flowers freely and scatters its seed, so maintaining the stock.

The swamp loosestrife *(Decodon verticillatus)* is valued for its autumn colouring. It is a shrubby North American plant of 1-1.8m (3-6ft) with narrow, willow-like leaves in whorls along the stems. In summer these are green but become rich crimson before falling in autumn. Tiny pink flowers of a tubular shape nestle in the leaf axils.

In late summer the cotton grasses *(Eriophorum angustifolium* and *E. vaginatum)* flower and these look like blobs of snow dangling between the heathers and mosses of the native bogs. They are widespread in the arctic so naturally hardy, but never tall. They are normally between 15-45cm (6-18in) tall, with grooved, sedge-like leaves and prominent clusters of nodding spikelets, packed with silky white hairs. This down was once used in Scotland as well as northern Europe for stuffing cushions and pillows.

Glyceria maxima, the manna grass, also has some economic importance in parts of eastern Europe on account of its seeds, which are greedily taken by geese and ducks, while the grass itself is relished by horses and other domesic animals. However, the only kind attractive enough for water gardens is the variegated form, correctly *G. maxima* variegata, although frequently sold as *G. spectabilis*. This very striking plant has broad, green, yellow and white stripes and suffusions on the leaves,

as well as touches of rosy-pink on the young foliage. It grows 45-60cm (18-24in) high, with taller plumes of brown grassy flowers in late summer. To retain the variegation it must be propagated by division in spring and not by seed.

Houttuynia cordata is a strange little plant, 15-25cm (6-10in) high with bluish-green, heart shaped leaves which when bruised emit a strong, rather unpleasant smell of oranges. The little white flowers have cone-shaped centres and there is a double form 'Plena'. Both are suitable for wet soil or shallow water, but they are invasive, spreading by means of creeping root-stocks, so they need to be kept in check quite ruthlessly.

Hypericum elodes, the marsh St John's wort is a lowly aquatic relative of the rose of Sharon and useful for masking pool edges since it is equally at home in boggy soil or

Yellow flags (Iris pseudacorus) *and the spring bloom of rhododendrons make a bright contrast with the more sombre hues of distant conifers.*

shallow water. It grows 15-23cm (6-9in) high and has leafy stems with small hairy foliage and soft yellow flowers.

Irises are well known garden and bulbous plants but there are also several that are true aquatics. Our native yellow flag, *Iris pseudacorus,* with rich yellow flowers on 60-100cm (24-36in) stems is one, and has varieties with primrose-yellow blooms like 'Bastardii' and one called 'Variegata' which is magnificent early in the year because of the heavy suffusion of gold on its foliage. This gives it a real sunshine appearance, but unfortunately the display does not last for very long and by mid-summer all the leaves become a more conventional plain green.

The yellow flag is said to have been the plant chosen by Louis VII for the French royal emblem during the Crusades, when it was called after him Fleur de Louis, then fleur-de-luce or fleur-de-lis. The roasted seeds have even been used as a substitute for coffee in times of scarcity.

Iris laevigata from Japan is one of the best blue-flowered water plants available and should be included in all planting schemes. It grows about 60-75cm (24-30in) tall with long grassy leaves and rich blue flowers with golden claw markings on their falls. It has produced a number of forms including a white called 'Alba'; 'Variegata' with white stripes on the foliage; 'Colchesteri' white with deep blue patterns and fall edgings; and 'Rose Queen', a hybrid with *I. kaempferi,* which is soft rose-pink. All these irises grow well in depths of 5-12.5cm (2-5in) of water and can be increased by division after flowering.

Most rushes are weedy plants not worthy of a place in small ornamental ponds. There is just one exception: the corkscrew rush, *Juncus effusus* 'Spiralis', which is fun to grow on account of its 45cm (18in) round, pithy stems, which are twisted like corkscrews for the whole of their length.

Ludwigias are creeping plants with smooth simple leaves, purple on the undersides, soft stems, and four-petalled yellow flowers. They can be used at pool margins and are also popular for aquaria.

The bog bean *(Menyanthes trifoliata)* takes its name from the three-parted leaves which are shaped something like those of a runner bean, although much thicker. They grow about 23cm (9in) high from creeping root-stocks, which also support clusters of pink and white flowers with pretty fringed petals. Like the bog arum it makes a good marginal plant for shallow water and for rather boggy soil.

Water forget-me-nots *(Myosotis palustris)* can be raised from seed and once established renew themselves naturally.

The deep blue 'Mermaid' is one of the best.

Nymphoides peltata is the water fringe, a trailer with clusters of golden, poppy-like flowers borne just clear of the water. The 5cm (2in) round, floating leaves have crinkled edges and are heavily mottled with chocolate blotches. The plant tends to run across water rather than grow upright but looks very pretty when in flower.

Orontium aquaticum is known as the golden club on account of its aroid flowers like white pokers with golden tips. It is an adaptable plant and will either grow in deep water, when the large, oblong leaves, waxy surfaced and velvety green, will float, or in shallow water when the stems toughen and leaves and flowers thrust upwards to a height of 30-45cm (12-18in). It must have deep soil and full sun to thrive and can be propagated from seeds as well as by division.

The North American arrow arums have, as their name implies, glossy arrow-shaped leaves and arum-like flowers. In *Peltandra sagittifolia* these are white and, if pollinated by insects, go on to produce red berries; whereas *P. virginica* has green flowers and green berries. They grow 30-50cm (12-

The green arrow arum (Peltandra virginica) *is a handsome, marsh-loving perennial with deep green, arrow-shaped leaves.*

Above *The pickerel weed* (Pontederia cordata) *has flowers that resemble miniature delphiniums.*

Opposite above Sagittaria sagittifolia, *also known as arrowhead, because of the shape of its aerial leaves, has white flowers with a deep purple centre.*

Opposite below Anemone narcissiflora *has white or cream-coloured flowers, occasionally flushed with pink.*

20in) tall according to soil conditions, which, for the best results, should be deep and fertile.

The pickerel weed *(Pontederia cordata)*, is an outstanding aquatic for late summer and a plant that rarely creates problems through being rampant. Yet it is a strong and upright grower with smooth and shining, heart-shaped leaves on long 45-60cm (18-24in) stems topped with 15cm (6in) spikes of closely packed, soft blue flowers set against a white, cottonwool-like background.

The seeds of pickerel weed were once enjoyed by American Indians, but are nowadays greedily taken by duck from areas where it grows plentifully, like quiet backwaters of the River Hudson. It is quite happy in a garden pond with about 15cm (6in) of water above its crowns.

Potentilla palustris, the marsh cinquefoil, is another creeping plant for pool margins; not particularly exciting but useful to cover bare, muddy areas. It has strawberry-like leaves, purple flowers and grows to a height of about 23-30cm (9-12in).

Preslia cervina, a small plant of 30cm (12in), with tiny, lance-shaped leaves and whorls of pinkish-mauve flowers, is chiefly remarkable for its strong, minty smell. It needs wet soil or very shallow water.

Most buttercups need damp soil but the spearwort, *Ranunculus lingua* 'Grandiflora', will take standing water several inches in depth. It is a handsome aquatic 60-100cm (24-36in) high, with large 7.5cm (3in) golden buttercups borne on wide, branching stems and very large, heart-shaped leaves 60-100cm (24-36in) across. It blooms intermittently through the summer.

Sagittarias are called arrowheads because of the shape of their aerial leaves. In running water these are grass-like and completely submerged. There are many kinds, some hardy, some tender, many quite small and a few large and decorative (although usually tender in Britain). Only one is striking enough to be planted in the pool and that is a double form of our native *S. sagittifolia* called 'Flore Pleno'. This has pure white rosettes so tightly packed together that the inflorescence bears some resemblance to a white double stock. It grows around 38-45cm (15-18in) high but is not as robust as the single species, so grow it in shallow water and a sheltered corner.

The lizard's tails *(Saururus cernuus* and *S. chinensis)* are curious little plants with thick aromatic rhizomes, heart-shaped leaves and nodding 10-12.5cm (4-5in) spikes of fragrant white flowers resembling little tails. Height is 30-60cm (12-24in).

The bullrush family of *Scirpus* is a large one, widely distributed all over the world on wet moors, bogs, and in streams. In Britain, the common name is often erroneously applied to *Typha* spp. (see below) but *Scirpus lacustris* is the true bullrush. At one time it was widely used for mats and chair seats and also eaten when young as a vegetable. The round, pithy stems are common in old pools but too invasive for gardens, where the only kinds worth growing are the zebra rush *(S. tabernaemontani* 'Zebrinus') which has its stems alternately and horizontally banded like porcupine quills in green and white, and *S. tabernaemontani* 'Albescens' with cream stripes running vertically up the stems. Both are extremely ornamental and can be kept colourful by removing the odd green rush if it appears.

Typhas, the reed maces are well-known aquatics with flat, sword-shaped leaves and oblong, poker-shaped heads of velvety brown flowers. These are often cut for dried flower arrangements in winter. The larger kinds should never be planted in an ornamental pool, otherwise they will soon oust every other plant. There is really only one that can be safely introduced and that is the dwarf species *T. minima*; it grows only 30-60cm (12-24in) high and has 7.5-12.5cm (3-5in) flower spikes. It is non-invasive and quite attractive for a small pool or as a tub. It is also suitable for dried flower arrangements.

The brooklime *(Veronica beccabunga)* is a rare native with blue forget-me-not flowers and smooth, elliptical leaves on 23-30cm (9-12in) stems. It flowers all through the early summer and makes a good associate for any of the other short aquatics like bog arums and bog beans.

Bog plants

Bog plants will increase the possibilities still further, and aid the transition between the pond and the rest of the garden. Some of the plants included here are well known as border plants, others are specialized bog plants that you will probably have to search out from a specialist supplier.

The genus *Anemone* is large and varied. Most species need well-drained and sunny situations, but there are some more suited to the damp soil of a bog garden. The following may be raised from seed or propagated by division in spring.

Anemone narcissiflora, grows to about 60cm (24in) and with its branching heads of white buttercup-like flowers bears some resemblance to an early summer Japanese anemone. *A. rivularis*, also about 60cm (24in) high has branched stems bearing white flowers with blue anthers and blue outsides. *A. virginiana*, the North American thimbleweed, grows 30-45cm (12-18in) high and has deeply cut leaves and a few white or greenish flowers.

The goat's beard *(Aruncus dioicus*, also known as *A. sylvester* and *Spiraea aruncus)* is one of the most imposing and, indeed, noble plants for the boggy margin of a pond. It produces heavy trusses of creamy white flowers, up to 1.8m (6ft) with a rich scent of hay, and deeply cut leaves on stems 1.2m (4ft) long. The seed heads may be used in dried flower arrangements. The plants are happy in moist situations in sun or partial shade and may be propagated by division in spring.

Astilbes are long-lived perennials that remain in flower for many weeks and, even when over, the dried seed heads are attractive for winter arrangements. The flowers are borne in tapering plumes and there are pink, crimson, and white varieties. The compound leaves, rather like those on a strawberry plant, make excellent ground cover and show off the feathery flower spikes to perfection. Astilbes grow well in

The astilbe hybrid 'White Queen' is a first-class plant for moist soils, bog gardens or pool-sides.

any good soil in sun or light shade provided they always have plenty of water around their roots.

Named varieties of astilbe are easily propagated by division; the species may be raised from seed. Many hybrids, to which several species have contributed, are grouped under the collective name of *A x arendsii*. They vary in height from 0.6-1.2m (2-4ft) down to 30-45cm (12-18in). Among the taller varieties are 'White Gloria'; 'Erica', bright pink; 'Bremen', salmon-crimson; 'Granat', deep crimson; and 'Koblenz', salmon. Short varieties include 'Praecox Alba', white; 'Sprite', soft pink; and the very late flowering, 'Serenade', clear pink. The white-flowered species *A. thunbergii*, has a bold, erect habit and does well in light shade.

Brunnera macrophylla, often catalogued as *Anchusa myosotidiflora*, is a splendid ground cover plant for a moist situation. It has rough, heart-shaped leaves and sprays of blue flowers like large forget-me-nots. It seeds freely and can be invasive unless checked. There is a variegated form.

The bugbanes, (*Cimicifuga* spp.), have strongly scented leaves reputed to discourage bugs, but are generally grown for their white feathery plumes of late summer flowers. These are carried on leafy stems about 1.5-1.8m (5-6ft) high. The deeply cut and divided leaves are attractive all summer. *C. racemosa* and *C. simplex*, with varieties of the last such as 'Elstead Variety' or 'White Pearl', are the best choice for small gardens.

The charming meadowsweet of watery meadows is *Filipendula ulmaria*. This attractive plant with its divided leaves and 60-100cm (24-36in) branching plumes of fragant, creamy flowers is beautiful enough to bring into the garden, along with its

varieties 'Variegata' with gold-splashed leaves and the golden-foliaged 'Aurea'. There are also pink-flowered species among which the North American *F. rubra* 'Venusta', which grows to 1.2-1.5m (4-5ft), and has fragrant, rosy flowers, is a particularly fine example.

Gentians are usually associated with rock gardens but some thrive in soil that is fairly moist at all times, like the drier areas of the bog garden. The willow gentian, *Gentiana asclepiadea*, with long willow-like leaves, has arching stems 60cm (24in) long with rich blue trumpet flowers; there is also an attractive white variety.

Gentiana lutea, the great yellow gentian, is an erect leafy perennial 1.2-1.8m (4-6ft) high. It has large, broadly ovate leaves and dense clusters of 2.5cm (1in) yellow flowers towards the ends of the stems. The root is used medicinally and in the preparation of vermouth.

No plant is more impressive at the boggy margin of a large pool than *Gunnera manicata*. It is a Brazilian species with the largest entire leaves of any land plant. These bear some resemblance to a giant rhubarb and can be 1.8-2.4m (6-8ft) across on stems 1.5-3m (5-10ft) high. Greenish-brown flowers appear in early summer in spikes which bear a strong resemblance to giant bottle brush cleaners. They are usually 1-1.2m (3-4ft) long. In winter the crowns of the plants must be protected from frost by cutting the leaves and inverting these over the crowns, adding a covering of straw or leaves in very exposed situations. *G. magellanica*, from the Falkland Islands and Patagonia, is a mat-forming species a mere 7.5cm (3in) high, which makes a good ground cover plant.

Although the hostas, or plantain lilies (formerly known as funkias) will grow happily in any reasonably fertile soil in sun or shade they are happiest and look best in semi-shaded moist soil by the side of water. There they make large-leaved imposing plants. They are herbaceous perennials, easily propagated by division in spring, although it is best to clip off sections from the outside of the clumps in order to avoid disturbing the parent plants.

Plantain lilies are mainly grown for their striking foliage, which may be light or dark green or gloriously variegated, edged or striped with white or golden yellow. They also have attractive spikes of flowers. These may be white, lilac to violet or rosy purple and are often sweetly scented. There are many species and varieties available including *H. fortunei*, green, with varieties *H.f.* 'Albopicta', with yellow leaves edged with green, and *H.f.* 'Marginatoa-alba', green with white-edged leaves; *H.*

sieboldiana has huge, glaucous green leaves and there are various other varieties with white leaf margins.

Mention busy Lizzies *(Impatiens)* and most of us think of the colourful, tender species *I. sultanii* and *I. holstii* and their hybrids and varieties. While these are easily raised from seed and look charming in a moist border beside the pond, they do have to be planted out each year, after all danger of frost is past.

Quite hardy however, is the giant balsam, *I. roylei* (syn. *I. glandulifera)* from the Himalayas, which is also known – like our native *I. noli-tangere* – as touch-me-not because, at a certain stage of ripeness, if you touch the pointed tip of the seed pod it will explode and scatter its seeds over an area of several feet. At a later stage, of course, it will do this naturally, a circumstance that has allowed it to spread along many river banks and streamsides, particularly in Wales and the south of England. The plant, which is a hardy annual, grows 1.2-1.8m (4-6ft) tall with thick, succulent stems carrying oval leaves and groups of large 5cm (2in) pink, red, crimson, or white flowers in the upper leaf axils.

Irises are almost indispensable for boggy margins and among the most outstanding are the many forms of the clematis-flowered *Iris kaempferi* from Japan. These like rich, lime-free soil and plenty of water during the growing season, but drier conditions in winter. Indeed they can be grown very successfully in an ordinary garden border if they are kept moist by flooding water over them in any dry spell in summer. The flowers are unique among irises in that the falls (popularly called petals) are held horizontally and so look something like a large clematis. There are white, cream, yellow, blue, violet, crimson, and reddish-purple forms, also many bicoloured varieties, and various doubles. They grow from 60-100cm (24-36in) and are propagated by division immediately after flowering.

These irises are sometimes confused with the truly aquatic *I. laevigata* varieties, but can easily be distinguished by feeling the leaves. Those of *I. kaempferi* have a prominent mid-rib, whereas *I. laevigata* leaves are uniformly flat.

Iris sibirica is one of those adaptable plants, able to do well in moist soil or dry. No special conditions are necessary except sun, but nowhere do they look better than at the water's edge, especially when duplicated by reflection. The plants form neat, tufted clumps of 60-100cm (24-36in) with grassy leaves and small, shapely flowers in various shades of blue as well as white and purple. Good varieties are

'Ottawa', bright blue; 'Roger Perry', deep blue; 'Alba', white; 'Helen Astor', rosy-red; and 'Caesar', rich purple. *I. versicolor* needs moist soil and sun and associates well with *I. sibirica.* It grows 60cm (24in) tall and has purplish-red flowers, deep wine red in the form *I.v.* 'Kermesina'.

Kirengeshoma palmata from Japan, commonly known as yellow waxbells, flowers late in the year just when the garden is beginning to lose its floral charm. It is happy in deep, moist soil, in light or deep shade. It grows to 1-1.2m (3-4ft). The leaves are shaped like those of a maple on black stems, while the soft yellow flowers, 5cm (2in) long and shaped like shuttlecocks, hang down in loose sprays. It is propagated by seed or division but resents root disturbance, so great care is necessary with the planting.

All the ligularias favour very moist ground, otherwise the foliage quickly flags. They have daisy-like flowers of yellow or orange but are also grown for their leaves, which may be deeply cut into finger-like segments in the 1.5m (5ft) Chinese *L. przewalskii*; large and heart-shaped in the 1.2m (4ft) *L. dentata* (also known as *Senecio clivorum)*; or kidney-shaped in the small, 1m (3ft) *L. hodgsonii.*

Vivid scarlet, perennial lobelias make a spendid and long-lasting display in a boggy waterside area. Three species, with their varieties and some hybrids, are commonly grown and all reach a height of about 1m (3ft). *L. cardinalis,* the cardinal flower, has rosettes of green leaves and brilliant scarlet

Below *The clematis-flowered Japanese* Iris kaempferi *flourishes near water.*

Bottom *Valued for its large, decorative leaves, the hosta, or plantain lily, boasts a range of foliage effects, including variegated patterns of green, silver and gold.*

flowers; *L. fulgens* has crimson stems and reddish leaves as well as scarlet flowers but is not reliably hardy. Accordingly, one should lift the plants and overwinter them under cover or else root a few from cuttings and keep these in a cold frame.

The blue cardinal flower *L. syphilitica* has dense spikes of blue flowers rather smaller than the others mentioned; there is also a white variety and hybrids with violet or crimson-violet flowers.

Lysichiton, often but erroneously called skunk cabbage (the true owner of this name is *Symplocarpus foetidus)*, shares with that plant unpleasantly scented flowers. There are two species, of which the North American *L. americanum* is the most arresting. The flowers come first, huge yellow arums each about 30cm (12in) high and are followed by quite massive, rich green leaves, up to 1.2m (4ft) high and 30cm (12in) across. The plant accordingly needs plenty of room, and does equally well in shallow water or wet boggy ground in sun. *L. camtschatcense* is similar but with pure white, rather smaller flowers and has no unpleasant scent. Propagation is usually by means of self-sown seed.

The purple loosestrifes *(Lythrum salicaria* and *L. virgatum)* flower in late summer and favour damp, low-lying areas. They may be propagated by division. *L. salicaria* grows 1.2m (4ft) or more high, and has linear to oblong leaves. The flower spikes carry many reddish-purple blossoms which glow in the afternoon sunlight. There are several named varieties of rosy-red or pink. *L. virgatum* has pink flowers and there is also a variety called 'Dropmore Purple'.

Meconopsis are members of the poppy family and make beautiful associates for primulas and ferns in cool, semi-shaded, moist conditions. They need an acid soil and do not like sodden ground – moist, but never waterlogged should be the aim. They need a fairly rich soil so a generous quantity of peat, leaf soil or garden compost should be worked in before planting. Meconopsis are propagated by seed sown immediately after harvesting or, in some cases, by division.

The best-loved kind is the blue poppy, *Meconopsis betonicifolia (*syn. *M. baileyi),* which grows to about 1.2m (4ft) and carries large, cup-shaped, rich blue flowers filled with masses of golden stamens.

Below Primula pulverulenta, *one of the candelabra primulas, makes a striking display when planted in large clumps.*

Below right *Striking in both form and colour,* Lysichitum americanum *flowers in the spring.*

The Welsh poppy *(M. cambrica)* loves moist conditions, although it will grow anywhere and, if allowed to seed itself, can be a joy in spring gardens. Apart from single yellow and orange flowers, there are also double forms, all of which may be raised from seed. They grow to 30-45cm (12-18in).

Other species of meconopsis are available from seedsmen, notably the yellow-flowered *M. regia* with handsome leaves that may be silver or golden because of a heavy covering of bristly hairs; *M. napaulensis* with red, purple or blue flowers and *M. x sheldonii,* blue and longer-lived than one of its parents, *M. betonicifolia.*

Mimulus species and hybrids make charming bog plants, although they will also grow in ordinary garden soil provided they are given sun and plenty of water. Forms of the monkey musk, *M. variegatus,* with large yellow or red-spotted flowers, are not reliably hardy and are usually raised from seed each year. *M. lewisii,* 30-60cm (12-24in) has rose-pink flowers from mid-summer to early autumn, and *M. cardinalis* of similar habit produces scarlet flowers. These species may be propagated by division in early or mid-spring, or by cuttings in mid or late spring.

Monarda didyma looks rather like a large dead nettle, except that its leaves are sweetly aromatic. These are made into tea in its native North America, a circumstance which accounts for such common names as bee balm and Oswego tea. The variety usually grown is 'Cambridge Scarlet', a brilliant red, with square, leafy stems 60-100cm (24-36in) high. 'Croftway Pink' is rose-pink and there are white and purplish varieties. Full sun and moist soil is essential, given which the plants soon spread.

The umbrella plant *(Peltiphyllum peltatum)* has earned this name because of the shape of its large, round leaves with their central stems. The flowers come first, very early in spring, rich pink and in round heads on 1m (3ft) stems. Wet ground is essential, but the plant is indifferent to sun or shade.

Few plants create a more beautiful feature in bog gardens than the Candelabra primulas. Most dislike standing water or sour conditions and are happiest when there is plenty of water lower down so that the soil around the roots is kept moist.

All primulas like good, rich soil. So work in garden compost, or well rotted manure at planting time and mulch generously with peat, mushroom compost or well decayed leaves each spring to conserve moisture in the top few inches of soil.

Some species like the dwarf *Primula* *rosea* 15-23cm (6-9in), with lovely clear, rose-pink flowers, can stand being submerged for short periods and enjoy really boggy conditions. *P. florindae,* the giant cowslip with umbels of fragrant, pendent, bell-shaped yellow flowers on 1-1.5m (3-5ft) stems, will also grow in really wet ground.

The most popular kinds for boggy areas, however, are the 'Candelabra' primulas, which carry their flowers in a series of tiers up their 60-100cm (24-36in) stems. These primulas include *P. beesiana,* with fragrant rosy carmine flowers; *P. bulleyana,* buff-orange; *P. helodoxa,* golden yellow; and *P. pulverulenta,* which has produced some outstanding varieties with apricot, buff, orange-red, rose-pink and salmon forms.

Another sturdy group comprises variously coloured varieties of *P. japonica* with white, pink, or crimson flowers.

Another excellent species is *P. denticulata,* the drumstick primula, which has round balls of white, lavender, purple, or carmine flowers. It grows 30-60cm (12-24in) high and is often seen in garden borders.

All these primulas may be raised from seed or may be propagated by root division in spring.

All the buttercups *(Ranunculus* spp.) are essentially moisture-loving plants; thriving in rather heavy soil in sun or light shade. *R. aconitifolius* has dark green, divided leaves and carries masses of single white flowers on stems about 60cm (24in) high; its double form, 'Flore Pleno', the white bachelor's buttons, the most garden-worthy, but does best in light shade. *R. acris* 'Flore Pleno', the yellow bachelor's buttons, growing to about 45cm (18in), is the double form of the European buttercup, and just as much of a sun lover.

Rheums are ornamental rhubarbs which, since they grow tall and have heavy plumes of flowers, make very imposing waterside plants. They need plenty of room as they can grow up to 3m (10ft). Most popular is *R. palmatum,* which has deeply cut leaves as large as those of the cultivated rhubarb. The fluffy flower spikes are white or pink; a variety called 'Atrosanguineum' is particularly fine, with red flowers and also red leaves early in the year. Rheums may be propagated by seed or division between late autumn and early spring.

Rodgersias, commonly known as Rodger's bronze leaf, are grown as much for their large leaves, which are divided like those of a horse-chestnut (round in the case of *R. tabularis),* and either bronzed or dark olive green, as for their flowers. The last produce long, feathery, astilbe-like plumes in the summer months.

Zantedeschia aethiopica, *the arum lily, can be grown outdoors in mild areas where its superb blooms will grace the outer reaches of any pool.*

Rodgersias need plenty of moisture and are happy in a bog garden, in ditches, or on stream banks. The following species all grow to about 1m (3ft): *R. pinnata,* pink; *R. podophylla, R. purdomii* and *R. sambucifolia* all have creamy white flowers and all have divided foliage, as does *R. aesculifolia,* which at 1.2m (4ft) is a litle taller and has branched sprays of cream or pink flowers. *R. tabularis* also has creamy-white flowers but its large, round, green leaves resemble parasols and are individually up to 1m (3ft) across.

Insectivorous plants are nearly all denizens of bogs and, while the majority are either too small or too tender to grow outside in Britain, *Sarracenia flava,* the North American pitcher plant, will often succeed in the milder counties. It has yellow leaves converted to traps for catching insects and nodding yellow flowers shaped like parachutes on 30cm (12in) stems. The purple *S. purpurea* has become naturalized in parts of Ireland. Both plants should have sphagnum moss and peat in their compost.

The kaffir lily (*Schizostylis coccinea*) resembles a small pink gladiolus, 30cm (12in) high. It needs sun and moist rather than wet soil. It flowers very late in the year, sometimes into late autumn.

The variegated form of our common figwort, *(Scrophularia aquatica* 'Variegata') retains its cream leaf and stem splashes all summer, so is a conspicuous bog plant well worth planting. It has nettle-shaped foliage, small chocolate-red flowers and grows 60cm (24in) tall. It is best increased from cuttings.

The globe flowers, *(Trollius* spp.) are related to buttercups and like the same conditions. They must never become dry at the roots, and are easily propagated by seed or division. Their leaves are attractive, being deeply divided and act as a charming foil to the large buttercup-like, yellow, golden or orange, globe-shaped flowers. The plants grow to about 60cm (24in) and are propagated by seed or division. Popular varieties are 'Orange Princess', 'Canary Bird', 'Golden Queen' and 'Earliest of All', all of them derived from *T. europaeus* and various Chinese species.

Arum lilies, *(Zantedeschia aethiopica)* are well-known South African plants with large and glossy, dark green, arrow-shaped leaves and 12.5-15cm (5-6in) pure white flowers with a golden pencil-shaped spadix inside each. In their native Africa they are commonly found in ditches and at the sides of pools, but in Britain they are best grown above water, preferably in the drier reaches of the bog. This is due to their need for dryness in winter. If it is not possible to meet these conditions, grow the tubers in large flower pots, sinking then into the soil in spring and storing them in a shed for winter. The hardiest variety, 'Crowborough', we have grown outside for over 20 years without protection, so they will flourish in Britain. The plant is best increased from small bulblets on the old plants.

Shrubs and trees

A certain number of permanent plants are necessary in the vicinity of any water garden, in order to provide shelter from strong or cold winds. A few shrubs will possibly answer in the case of small to medium-sized gardens but, for large exposed areas, trees may prove more effective and satisfactory.

Where the ground is naturally very moist or is liable to occasional flooding, many garden trees and shrubs are unlikely to prove successful. The following, however, are reasonably tolerant of wet, some more than others – like alders and any of the willows. Most bamboos will also grow well in damp soil, as well as trees like metasequoias and taxodiums.

If room permits, *Acer rubrum,* the swamp maple, is of value for its autumn leaf colourings of scarlet and orange, but it will grow 21m (70ft) or more in height. Alders such as *Alnus glutinosa* will take very wet conditions and have attractive catkins early in the year.

Hydrangeas always do well beside water, provided the roots are not submerged; spiraeas need sun and moist soil to produce their feathery sprays of small white or crimson flowers, while the taller *Sorbaria aitchisonii* and *S. arborea,* 1.8-2.4m (6-8ft) and 3-6m (10-20ft) respectively, carry massive plumes of creamy-white florets in late summer.

Provided the soil is not limy, *Pernettya mucronata,* an evergreen shrub from Chile, will prove a real asset for acid bog gardens. The 0.6-1.5m (2-5ft) bushes have narrow leaves with spiny tips and small nodding white flowers which, when pollinated, go on to form marble-sized berries of white, pink, purple, red and near black. However, since male and female flowers are borne on separate plants it is necessary to have one male plant to every five or six female.

If more colour is wanted in the bog garden, it is a good idea to introduce a few bulbs in the drier regions, selecting kinds that will spread naturally. Examples are snowdrops, narcissi, bluebells, erythroniums; also camassias, which have slender spikes of blue flowers and grow 1m (3ft) tall in early summer. Try a few of these at first in different positions to assess their suitability.

INDEX

Picture Credits

Front cover: Steve Bicknell   **Back cover:** Marshall Cavendish Library

A–Z Collection: 43; Amateur Gardening: 5; Heather Angel: 47(t,br), 51(c); D. Arminson: 57; Ed Baxter: 21, 22; Steve Bicknell: 2/3, 38; D. Blog: 62; Alan Bloom: 13; Bruce Coleman Ltd.: 44; R. J. Corbin: 36, 41, 49(t,cl), 50(br), 51(tr), 67(b); Valerie Finnis: 37, 50(bl), 65(b); Brian Furner: 40; S. Grub: 55(t,cl,bl,bc,br); J. Hovell: 20; Bill Howes: 50(tr); P. Hunt: 61(cr), 68(r); George Hyde: 31, 47(bl); Leslie Johns: 66; L'Ami des Jardines: 51(tl); Lotus Water Garden Products Ltd.: 8, 25, 29, 32; J. Markham: 50(tl), 58(r), 59, 65(t); L. Hugh Newman: 49; M. Newton: 35; R. Procter: 33, 50(c), 64; Ianthe Ruthven: 10/1; Harry Smith Collection: 1, 7, 9, 10, 11, 55(cr), 56, 60, 63, 67(t), 68(l); Spectrum Colour Library: 4; Stapeley Water Gardens: 15, 18, 48(t,b); Clive Streeter: 26, 28, 30; C. Tandy: 12; Transworld Feature Syndicate Inc.: 23; Trevor Vertigan: 19.